THE LITTLE RED BOOK
of
COMMON ERRORS

By the same author

Little Red Book Series

Little Red Book of Slang-Chat Room Slang	Little Red Book of Synonyms
Little Red Book of English Vocabulary Today	Little Red Book of Antonyms
Little Red Book of Grammar Made Easy	Little Red Book of Common Errors
Little Red Book of English Proverbs	Little Red Book of Letter Writing
Little Red Book of Prepositions	Little Red Book of Essay Writing
Little Red Book of Idioms and Phrases	Little Red Book of Word Fact
Little Red Book of Effective Speaking Skills	Little Red Book of Language Checklist
Little Red Book of Phrasal Verbs	Little Red Book of Perfect Written English
Little Red Book of Euphemisms	Little Red Book of Punctuation
Little Red Book of Word Power	Little Red Book of Reading and Listening
Little Red Book of Modern Writing Skills	Little Red Book of A Child's First Dictionary

A2Z Book Series

A2Z Quiz Book	A2Z Book of Word Origins

Others

The Book of Fun Facts The Book of More Fun Facts The Book of Firsts and Lasts The Book of Virtues World Facts Finder	The Book of Motivation Read Write Right: Common Errors in English The Students' Companion
Fun Facts: Science Fun Facts: Animals Fun Facts: India Fun Facts: Nature	Fun with Maths Fun with Numbers Fun with Puzzles Fun with Riddles

THE LITTLE RED BOOK *of* COMMON ERRORS

Terry O'Brien

RUPA

Published by
Rupa Publications India Pvt. Ltd 2012
7/16, Ansari Road, Daryaganj
New Delhi 110002

Sales centres:
Bengaluru Chennai
Hyderabad Jaipur Kathmandu
Kolkata Mumbai Prayagraj

Copyright © Terry O' Brien 2012

All rights reserved.
No part of this publication may be reproduced, transmitted,
or stored in a retrieval system, in any form or by any means,
electronic, mechanical, photocopying, recording or otherwise,
without the prior permission of the publisher.

P-ISBN: 978-81-291-1970-4
E-ISBN: 978-81-291-2179-0

Nineteenth impression 2024

20 19

The moral right of the author has been asserted.

Typeset by Innovative Processors, New Delhi

Printed in India

This book is sold subject to the condition that it shall not, by way of
trade or otherwise, be lent, resold, hired out, or otherwise circulated,
without the publisher's prior consent, in any form of binding or cover
other than that in which it is published.

Given below are certain abbrevations that have been used in the book:

- **✗** Provides an example of the incorrect or inappropriate use of the appropriate word.

- **✓** Provides an example of the correct or appropriate use of the word.

- **C** Offers an explanation.

NOUNS

Nouns omitted after Adjectives

Incorrect:	He went with his elder.
Correct :	He went with his elder brother.
Incorrect:	Please give me some blotting.
Correct :	Please give me some blotting paper.
Incorrect :	He lives in a boarding.
Correct:	He lives in a boarding-house.

NOTE: Elder is used with a possessive pronoun to mean one who is older as 'He is my elder' (=he is older than I am). It is also used as a noun with *the*, as 'He is the elder of the two'; 'By six years the elder of Sandeepa.'

Freeship for 'free-studentship,' earlihood for 'boyhood', or early life, are mere coined words.

Nouns omitted after Verbs

Incorrect:	He wished me.
Correct:	He wished me good morning, etc.
Incorrect:	I beg you.
Correct:	I beg your pardon.

PLURAL FOR SINGULAR

Common examples of this error are—

Rices, corns (grain), foods, cattles, furntures, mischiefs, filths, dirts, needleworks, woodworks, machineries, hairs, advices, preys, behaviours, poetries, abuses, sceneries, clergies, fuels, issues (progeny) off springs, youngs, peoples (persons), alphabets, sweats, logics, alarms, tributes, gouts (the disease).

Incorrect:	The sceneries of Switzerland are very fine.
Correct:	The scenery of Switzerland is very fine.
Incorrect:	Natives of India have black hairs.
Correct:	Natives of India have black hair.
Incorrect:	He gave me many good advices.
Correct:	He gave me much good advice.

NOTE: Rices, corns, foods, etc., are used only when different varieties of rice, corn, food, etc., are intended. We say a house is built of brick or of stone; not bricks or stones.

Cattle, prey, clergy, people in the sense of 'persons' (with vermin, poultry, gentry), being plural already in sense, have no plural form.

Needleworks and woolworks could only mean places where needles and wool were manufactured; cf." brickworks.'

Hairs are found in poetry for hair. Hairs is used in prose when attention is called to the number of hairs:—' I found several grey hairs on my head this morning.'

Advices is used, especially in mercantile language, in the sense of 'notification':—'From advices just received from our Mumbai firm we learn that the price of rice has risen.'

Abuses means evil or corrupt practices; it should not be used to denote terms of abuse.

Logic, with arithmetic, music, magic, and physic in the sense of medicine, filth, prey, dirt, sweat, gout, poetry, scenery, young, with offspring and issue in the sense of 'progeny,' are never used in the plural.

SINGULAR FOR PLURAL

Incorrect:	Please pass order for his release.
Correct:	Please pass orders for his release.
Incorrect	This amounts to two and three fourth.
Correct:	This amounts to two and three fourths.
Incorrect:	He does not like vegetable.
Correct:	He does not like vegetables.
Incorrect:	My circumstance will not allow my pursuing my study.
Correct:	My circumstances will not allow my pursuing my studies.

POSSESSIVE ENDING OMITTED

Incorrect:	The hero's death is different from the martyr.
Correct:	The hero's death is different from the martyr's.

A Singular Collective noun referred to by a plural pronoun.

Incorrect:	The firm has given a bonus to each of their clerks,
Correct:	The firm has given a bonus to each of its clerks.

POSSESSIVE CASE MISUSED

Incorrect:	He went out by the house's door.
Correct:	He went out by the door of the house.
Incorrect :	I shall go by the twelve o'clock's train.
Correct :	I shall go by the twelve o'clock train.

Similarly, 'Easter's holidays,' 'Eden's gardens', 'Monday's night, 'holiday's dress,' 'Puja's clothes,' are incorrect for' Easter holidays; ' 'Eden gardens, ' 'Monday night, ' 'holiday dress,' 'Puja clothes'.

NOTE: In the above instances we cannot substitute the form with of; we cannot say 'the holidays of Easter,' etc.

But 'on the night of Monday, the 2nd of June' is correct. So 'the summer vacation,' not 'the vacation of summer'; 'the winter term,' not 'the term of winter; 'a sea-fog,' 'a fog of the sea,' etc.

Water for Climate

| Incorrect: | The water of Noida does not suit my health. |
| Correct: | The clime of Noida does not suit my health |

Nouns incorrectly used

Incorrect:	The hall is full, there is no place for any more.
Correct:	The hall is full, there is no room for any more.
Incorrect:	He had a severe loss while running down stairs.
Correct:	He had a severe fall while running down stairs.
Incorrect:	Good night, Sir; I am glad you have come.
Correct:	Good evening, Sir; I am glad you have come.
Incorrect:	I have a private business with you.
Correct:	I have a private piece of business with you.
Incorrect:	He is seeking for an employment under Government.
Correct:	He is seeking for some employment under Government.

Incorrect:	He is one of my members.
Correct:	He is a member of my family.
Incorrect:	Credit it in my name.
Correct:	Credit it to my account.

NOTE: Good night is a parting salutation; Good morning, Good day, Good afternoon, Good evening are either meeting or parting salutations. In 'This is a bad business,' business means matter, event. **'o'clock' inserted**.

Incorrect:	I am going by the 12.30 o' clock train.
Correct:	I am going by the 12.30 train.

NOTE: When the number of minutes is specified, o'clock is not used.

The same word as both Subject and Object.

Incorrect:	This result I much regretted, and taught me a lesson for the future.
Correct:	This result I much regretted and it taught me a lesson for the future.
Incorrect:	An action which it is easy to blame, but is quite natural.
Correct :	An action which it is easy to blame, but which is quite natural.
Incorrect:	What a boy learns and is taught him are not the same thing.
Correct:	What a boy learns and what is taught him are not the same thing.
Incorrect:	What I have said is true, and I will not withdraw.

Correct:	What I have said is true, and I will not withdraw it.

Protagonist for Advocate

Incorrect:	He is a strong protagonist of democracy.
Correct :	He is a strong advocate of democracy.

NOTE: A protagonist is the leader in a business or the champion of a cause. The word is not antithetical to antagonist, and there cannot be a chief protagonist or several protagonists in a business or a cause.

Individual for Man, Person

Incorrect:	This is the same individual that came yesterday.
Correct:	This is the same man that came yesterday.

NOTE: Individual is correctly used of a single, separate person, as opposed to a number of persons, as while the community gains by Free Trade, the 'Individual sometimes loses.'

Mediocrity for Impartiality

Incorrect:	As a judge, he is conspicuous for his mediocrity.
Correct:	As a judge, he is conspicuous for his impartiality.

Quantity for Number

Incorrect:	I have lent him a quantity of books.
Correct:	I have lent him a number of books.

A Phrase treated as a Compound

Incorrect:	He enquired about your state of health.
Correct:	He enquired about the state of your health.
Incorrect:	He is an undoubted man of genius.
Correct:	He is a man of undoubted genius.

NOTE: In the same way, 'England's height of power' is wrong for 'the height of England's power'; 'Shakespeare's immortal creations of fancy ' for 'the immortal creations of Shakespeare's fancy'; 'his English knowledge' for 'his knowledge of English.' -

A Singular Collective noun with a plural pronoun or verb.

Incorrect:	The firm has given a bonus to each of their clerks.
Correct:	The firm has given a bonus to each of its clerks.
Incorrect:	The whole band, who had murdered its officers, were arrested yesterday.
Correct:	The whole band, who had murdered its officers, was arrested yesterday.

NOTE: Other examples of this error are: 'The Congress Party, through their leaders, has recognised the grievance' (Nation).

Tribute (to) for Proof (of)

Incorrect:	This repayment is a tribute to the honesty of the firm.
Correct:	This repayment is a proof of the honesty of the firm

Converse for Reverse

Incorrect:	His behaviour was the very converse of polite.
Correct:	His behaviour was the very reverse of polite.

NOTE: Converse implies a reciprocal relation between two opposites 'Intellect without wealth is the converse of wealth without intellect'; reverse connotes mere contrariety.

Audience for Spectators

Incorrect:	The dumb show drew a numerous audience.
Correct:	The dumb show drew numerous spectators.

NOTE: Similarly 'the songs of the angels were beyond the reach of her vision (hearing)'; 'The crowd was so large that it visibly (sensibly) increased the heat.' So in 'The sad faces and joyous music formed an incongruous sight' substitute combination for sight, since music cannot be seen.

Etc. (or &c.) inserted

Do not write:	His career was marred by ill health, poverty, etc.
Write:	His career was marred by ill health, poverty, and other misfortunes.

NOTE: Etc. is out of place in literature, and should be confined to business communications and familiar letters.

ADJECTIVES

Staple for, Standard

Incorrect:	These are staple works on Indian history.
Correct:	These are standard works on Indian history.

Unique for Sole or Peculiar

Incorrect:	This is the unique cause of my failure.
Correct:	This is the sole cause of my failure.
Incorrect:	There is something unique in his dealing with the case.
Correct:	There is something peculiar in his dealing with the case.

Future for Subsequent

Incorrect:	The future proceedings did not interest me.
Correct:	The subsequent proceedings did not interest me.

Prolific for Frequent

Incorrect:	This is a prolific cause of delay.
Correct:	This is a frequent cause of declay.

Mutual for Common

Incorrect:	We two were talking about our mutual liking for olives.
Correct:	We two were talking about our common liking for olives.

NOTE: 'Our mutual affection' = the affection that we both feel for each other, Our common affection '= the affection that we both feel for someone else. 'Our mutual friend' is thus incorrect.

Mutual for Reciprocal

Incorrect:	Since I helped you, I hope you will give me mutual help.
Correct:	Since I helped you, I hope you will give me reciprocal help.

NOTE: Two persons can have mutual or reciprocal feelings towards each other; but one person cannot have mutual, but only reciprocal, feelings towards the other.

Mutual for Simultaneous

Incorrect:	They were seen on the day of their parents' mutual disappearance.
Correct:	They were seen on the day of their parents' simultaneous disappearance.

Feasible for Possible or Probable

Incorrect:	He said it was quite feasible that the car was stolen.
Correct:	He said it was quite possible that the car was stolen.
Incorrect:	This is a feasible conjecture of what happened.
Correct:	This is a probable conjecture of what happened.

Probable for Likely

Incorrect:	No dispute is probable to arise between them.
Correct:	No dispute is likely to arise between them.

NOTE: Similarly is possible to arise is wrong, write 'can arise' or 'can possibly arise.' The future should not be used after probable'.

Oblivious for Unaware, Unconscious

Incorrect:	He went off, quite oblivious of the fact that he had dropped his purse.
Correct:	He went off, quite unaware of the fact etc.

NOTE: Oblivious means 'no longer aware,' not simply 'unaware.'

Not any for No

Incorrect:	There is not any snake in Iceland.
Correct:	There are no snakes in Iceland.
Incorrect:	Any one cannot do this.
Correct:	No one can do this.

NOTE: 'Not everyone can do this' is preferable to 'Every one cannot do this.' Observe that—not every =some; not any = none. Both the following are correct.

(1) I could not find anybody there.

(2) I could find nobody there.

'Other' (1) omitted after a Comparative, or (2) inserted after a Superlative, or (3) wrongly omitted

Incorrect:	Chandrgupt was wiser than all the Indian kings
	Chandrgupt was wiser than all the other Indian kings.
Correct:	Chandrgupt was the wisest of all the Indian kings.

Incorrect:	Of all other kings Chandrgupt was the wisest.
	Of all kings Chandrgupt was the wisest.
Correct:	Chandrgupt was wiser than all other kings.

NOTE: 'Of all others I like a boy that tells the truth' should be 'More than all others I like a boy' etc., or 'Most of all I like a boy' etc. Similarly, 'Homer is the finest poet of anybody in the world' should be 'Homer is a finer poet than anybody else in the world.'

Incorrect:	Winter is a hard time for birds and bipeds.
Correct:	Winter is a hard time for birds and other bipeds.

NOTE: Simflarly, 'Mazzini did more for Italy than any living man.' should be 'any other.

Less for Fewer

Incorrect:	There are no less than ten books here.
Correct:	There are no fewer than ten books here.

N0TE.—Fewer denotes number, less denotes quantity or degree :—' fewer mangoes, 'less rice.' But we say 'I will not take less than ten rupees,' because the ten rupees are regarded as a sum of money and not as a number of coins.

Latter for Last

Incorrect:	He brought pen, ink, and paper, the latter being foolscap.
Correct:	He brought pen, ink, and paper, the last being foolscap.

NOTE: *Latter* should be confined to the second of two things previously mentioned :—' He brought pen and ink, the latter in a small bottle.'

The Superlative for the Comparative

Incorrect:	This is the wisest plan of the two.

| Correct: | This is the wiser plan of the two. |

NOTE: But the Superlative is often used colloquially of two things like this best of the two,'' Of two evils choose the least.

Superlatives in '-est 'for Positives with 'very' 'most.'

Incorrect:	This is a best blook.
Correct:	This is a very good book.
Incorrect:	They made a fiercest attack on him.
Correct:	They made a most fierce attack on him.

NOTE: The superlative in -*est* must never be used after the indefinite article. It always implies comparison: thus 'This is the best book' implies that this book is better than any of certain books with which it is compared.

Comparatives in '-er' with ' more'; Superlatives in '-est' with ' most.'

Incorrect:	This road is more shorter than that.
Correct:	This road is shorter than that.
Incorrect:	This road is the most shortest of all.
Correct:	This road is the shortest of all.

NOTE: We may however, say 'This is a far shorter road than that'; 'This is the very shortest road.'

Positive Degree with 'than 'for Comparative

| Incorrect: | This stick is long than that. |

Correct :	This stick is longer than that.
Incorrect:	We learnt a great deal than the others.
Correct :	We learnt a great deal more than the others.

Than 'for 'to' after 'superior,' 'inferior,' etc.

| Incorrect: | This paper is superior than that. |
| Correct: | This paper is superior to that. |

NOTE: A similar mistake is more preferable than for preferable than for preferable to.

Positive Degree coupled by 'and' to Superlative

| Incorrect: | He enjoyed all the sweetest and charming scenery. |
| Correct: | He enjoyed all the sweetest and most charming scenery. |

ERRORS IN THE CHOICE OF WORDS

Words Often Misused

Some words suffer from constant '**abusage**'. They are used with the wrong meaning or misused grammatically. Here is a list of some mistakes of this kind, with the corrections supplied.

1. **Above** for **foregoing** or **preceding**

    - ✗ The **above** remarks apply to all students.
    - ✓ The **preceding** remarks (or the remarks given/mentioned above) apply to all students.
    - C *Above* is not an **adjective**.

2. **Aggravate** for **annoy**

    - ✗ That **aggravating** boy makes me see red!
    - ✓ The hot weather **aggravated** his illness.
    - C *Aggravate* means '**make worse**' and is generally used with an object.

3. **Centre** for **middle**

    - ✗ He parts his hair in the **centre**.
    - ✓ This is the **centre** of the circle.

> **C** *Centre* is a '**definite point**'; *middle* is the '**indefinite space**' around or near the centre.

4. Climax for crisis

> **✗** This difficult and dangerous political situation marked a *climax* in the nation's history.
>
> **✓** He reached the *climax* of his acting career with a brilliant performance on television.
>
> **C** *Climax* is the '**highest point**', *crisis* is the '**turning point**'.

5. Firstly for first

> **✗** **Firstly** I have no money, secondly I have no time.
>
> **✓** **First** I have no money, secondly I have no time.
>
> **C** *Firstly* is not a word of English.

6. Consider as for consider

> **✗** Please **consider** me as your friend.
>
> **✓** Please **consider** me your friend.
>
> **C** This mistake is perhaps caused by confusion with *regard* which takes as, e.g. Please regard me as you friend.

7. Coward for cowardly

- ✗ He is a **coward** man.
- ✓ He is a **cowardly** man.
- C *Coward* is a **noun**, the **adjective** of which is *Cowardly*.

8. Deny for refuse

- ✗ He **denied** my offer of help.
- ✓ He **refused** my offer of help and denied that he needed it.
- C *Deny* is to answer in the negative or to say that something is not true; *refuse* is not to take what is offered or not to do what one is asked to do.

9. Diligent for hard-working

- ✗ This **diligent** student will pass his examination.
- ✓ This **hard-working** student will pass his examination.
- C *Diligent* is considered literary a **scholarly** word, not often used today.

10. Explain *me* for explain to me

- ✗ Please **explain me** this exercise.
- ✓ Please **explain** this exercise **to me**.
- C Mistakes in syntax

11. Fairly for rather

x Shut the window; it is **fairly** cold.

✓ Shut the window; it is **rather** cold.

C **Fairly** and *rather* both mean *somewhat*, but *fairly* is used when we wish to express a pleasant or **desirable idea**, and *rather* when we wish to express an unpleasant or **undesirable idea**, e.g. The room is *fairly* big and I can put all my things in it. The room is *rather* big and I'm sure it will be draughty and uncomfortable.

Notice that *rather* as an understatement for *very* is used with both pleasant and unpleasant ideas, e.g. You are *rather* clever to do this.

12. Far for a long way

x He lives **far** from the station.

✓ He lives a **long way** from the station.

C Far is used:
(i) in **interrogative** and **negative** sentences.
(ii) in the expressions — *how far, so far, too far, as far*

In other cases it is replaced by a long way.

13. Habit for custom

- ✗ Drinking tea is an English **habit**.
- ✓ Drinking tea is an English **custom**.
- C *Habit* is for **individuals**, *custom* is for a country or **society**, it is a widely accepted way of behaving in a society; *Habit* means 'regular tendency'.

14. Individual for person

- ✗ A queer-looking **individual** came to our house.
- ✓ This book is about the claims of society upon the **individual**.
- C *Individual* means '**a single human being**' as opposed to family or society.

15. Intriguing for interesting, exciting curiosity

- ✗ What **intriguing** writing paper you use! I have never seen any like it.
- ✓ The **intriguing** plotters were discovered and killed.
- C *Intrigue* means '**trick**', '**deceive**', '**plot against**' and not '**arouse interest**' or '**curiosity**'.

16. Invent for discover

✗	Columbus **invented** America.
✓	Columbus **discovered** America.
C	'Invent' means 'to make or design something that did not exist before.' 'Discover' refers 'to the finding of a place or thing that already exists.' Therefore, the term '**discover**' is used here.

17. Issue for give

✗	The soldiers were **issued** with new boots.
✓	Blood was **issuing** from his mouth.
C	*Issue* means **come out**, **emerge**, **result**. The nouns *outcome, result, progeny* are also flagrantly misused, especially in journalese, where they are employed very loosely to mean matter, affair, discussion, question or conclusion.

18. Lend for borrow

✗	May I **lend** your umbrella? Mine is at home.
✓	May I **borrow** your umbrella? Mine is at home.

> **C** *Lend* is to '**give temporarily to**'; *borrow* is to **get temporarily from**, e.g., We **borrow** books from a lending library.

19. Literally for figuratively speaking

> **✗** (a) They **literally** flooded the place with pamphlets and papers.
>
> (b) His eyes **literally** devoured the scene.

> **✓** He translated the poem **literally** and did not attempt a free rendering.

> **C** Clearly, in the first two sentences, the word literally should not be used and 'flooded' and 'devoured' must not be taken literally but metaphorically or the results will be quite absurd.

20. Materialise for happen

> **✗** Don't worry about another war; it may never **materialise**.

> **✓** We waited for the ghost, but it failed to **materialise**.

> **C** *Materialise* means '**take bodily shape**'.

21. Measure for a certain amount or quantity

> **✗** He speaks with a **measure** of hesitation.

- ✓ I bought a kg of bananas and the greengrocer gave me a good **measure**.
- C Hesitation is a ***quality*** which cannot be quantified.

22. **Mutual** for **common**

- ✗ At that time France and England had a **mutual** enemy in Germany.
- ✓ My cousin and I enjoy the **mutual** benefits of a shared television set.
- C Fowler writes, 'mutual is a well-known trap. The essence of its meaning is that it involves the relation, x is or does to y as y to x; and not the relation, x is or does to z as y to z; from which it follows that our mutual friend Jones (meaning Jones who is your friend as well as mine) and all similar phrases are misuses.'

23. **Obey to** for **obey**

- ✗ Children should **obey to** their parents.
- ✓ Children should **obey** their parents.
- C The noun ***obedience*** is followed by '**to**', but **not** the verb *obey*.

24. **Open** and **shut** for **turn on** and **turn off** (*taps, lights, gas, radio, television*)

> ✗ He **shut** the radio, then **opened** the taps for his bath.
>
> ✓ He **turned off** the radio, then **turned on** the taps for his bath.
>
> C *To open* means to move something (e. g. a door, a window) so as to lower space, *shut* means to move something to block an upcoming.

25. Play for game

> ✗ They had a good **play** of football.
>
> ✓ They had a good **game** of football.
>
> C *Play* (an uncountable noun here) is the general word **for the action of sport**; game (countable) is a **particular spell of play**. *Play* is also used as a verb usually with *game*, e.g., We played this game until the rain stopped play.

26. Practically for almost or nearly

> ✗ I'm coming; I've **practically** finished.
>
> ✓ Theoretically it seems right, but **practically** it does not work.
>
> C *Practically* means '**in a practical manner**' or '**in practice**'.

27. Reaction for opinion, view, attitude, feeling, action, effect or influences

> ✗ His observations on space-travel had a **reaction** on every continent.
>
> When I read the news, my **reaction** was hostile.
>
> ✓ Last night he was excited; now, by way of **reaction**, he is depressed.
>
> C *Reaction* means
>
> (i) responsive or reciprocal action,
>
> (ii) return of previous condition after interval of opposite or
>
> (iii) (chiefly political) counter-stroke or retrograde tendency.

28. Remember for Remind

> ✗ Please **remember** me to bring some cakes.
>
> ✓ Please **remind** me to bring some cakes.
>
> C *Remember* means '**to have in mind**'; *remind* means '**to make one remember**'. In letters, 'Remember me kindly to your parents' means 'I send greetings to your parents'.

29. Robbed for stole

- ✗ They **robbed** a bicycle from him.
- ✓ They **stole** a bicycle from him.
- C The object of *steal* is the thing taken by the thief, e.g., a bicycle, jewellery, money. The object of *rob* is the person or place from whom or which the thing is taken, e.g., a millionaire, a house, a bank.

30. Shortly for Briefly

- ✗ He wrote **shortly** because he had very little paper.
- ✓ He wrote **briefly** because he had very little paper.
- C *Shortly* refers to **time**, and *briefly* to **manner**.

  e.g., I will write shortly (soon); and I will write not briefly but fully.

31. Sick for Ill

- ✗ He has been **sick** for three years now.
- ✓ He has been **ill** for three years now.
- C '**To be ill**' means '**to be in bad health**'. '**To be sick**' means 'to vomit',

or **'to be temporarily indisposed'**.

Sick can be used before a noun, or as a noun in the plural, e.g., We visit the sick; and they are grateful, especially the sick children. ***Ill*** cannot be used in this way. We must say 'The man who is ill', not 'The ill man'.

32. Tell for Say

> ✗ He **said** a lot of lies, and then went without telling me goodbye.

> ✓ He **told** a lot of lies, and then went without saying goodbye to me.

> C ***Tell*** means to **give information** (the truth, lies, stories, the time) or to calculate, to distinguish or to order.

Say is used for **actual words as they are spoken**, or for their meaning in indirect speech. Notice however, that when we say in direct speech it is followed by an object, 'tell' replaces it in indirect speech. e.g., "He said to his daughter, You are very silly." (**Direct**)

He told his daughter that she was very silly. (**Indirect**)

33. Thank you for no, thank you

> ✗ More tea? **Thank you**. (I don't want any more.)

- ✓ More tea? **No, thank you**. (I don't want any more.)

- C *Thank you* alone has **neither a negative nor an affirmative** implication. It is therefore necessary to make your answer clear by saying 'No, thank you' or 'Yes; thank you.'

34. Too for very

- ✗ The weather is **too** hot—I enjoy it like this.

- ✓ The weather is **very** hot—I enjoy it like this.

- C *Too* has the meaning of excess. It means 'very' only in such hyperbolic expressions as '*too* beautiful for words', 'you're too kind', etc.

35. Transpire for happen or occur

- ✗ This **transpired** to be the last football game of the season.

- ✓ If these secret conditions should **transpire**, your life will be in danger.

- C *Transpire* means 'to come to be known', or 'to prove to be the case'; To use it in the sense of '*to happen*' or '*occur*' is not very appropriate.

36. Unique for exceptional, peculiar or unusual

✗ 'A very **unique** child, thought I.' (Charlotte Bronte.)

✓ This event is unique in history.

C *Unique* means 'having no equal' or 'parallel' and cannot admit degrees of comparison.

37. Verbal for oral

✗ She had no time to write, so she sent a **verbal** message to her son.

✓ He is a master of words; his **verbal** subtleties are magnificent.

C *Verbal* means '**merely of**', or 'concerned with', and implies no distinction between spoken and written words.

38. What have you? for What is the matter?

✗ You are very pale; **what have you** this morning?

✓ You are very pale; **what is the matter** with you this morning?

C ***What have you*** is used to inquire about *what one has*, and not in, *what condition one is*.

39. Win for beat

> ✗ We always **win** your team at cricket.
> ✓ We always **beat** your team at cricket.
>
> C *Win* is to **gain something** for which you have tried (a prize, approval, a game, a battle); *beat* is to **overcome an opponent**, e.g., The girls beat the boys and won a silver cup.
>
> Notice that '**to get a win**' and '**to get a beating**' are opposites.

COMMON ERRORS

Errors in Parts of Speech

In this section we shall discuss erroneous usage of parts of speech inevitable for those students whose mother-tongue is not English. However, all may be prone to such mistakes.

NOUNS

1. ✗ The magistrate issued **order** for his arrest.

   ✓ The magistrate issued **orders** for his arrest.

   C **Orders** in this sense should always be used in the **plural**, e.g., Orders for expulsion, orders for execution, orders for promotion, orders for dismissal, etc.

2. ✗ My father is leaving for Delhi by the **8-30 o'clock** bus.

   ✓ My father is leaving for Delhi by the 8:30 bus.

   C **Don't** use 'o'clock' when **minutes are also mentioned**, e.g. 'by the 9:45 train', but 'by the 9 o'clock train'.

3. ✗ He has built a new **home** for himself.

   ✓ He has built a new **house** for himself.

   C Whereas a **house** is **any building** meant for residence, a **home** is a place of **residence with long associations**. A 'home' may also mean 'one's country'.

4. ✗ His **family members** are coming by this train.

   ✓ The **members of** his **family** are coming by this train.

   C The **correct** usage is **a member of the family**, not 'a family member'.

5. ✗ **Good night**, Rita; where have you been all these days?

   ✓ **Good evening**, Rita; where have you been all these days?

   C It is sometimes forgotten that, '**good night**' is a **parting salutation**, '**good evening**' is the proper **salutation** to be used when two people meet for the first time in the evening. One cannot make any further conversation after saying 'good night'.

6. ✗ He has already **cheated me twice** or thrice.

| ✓ | He has already **cheated on me** two or three times. |

| C | Though *twice* means 'two times' and *thrice* 'three times', they are formal and literary expressions and are not in everyday use. |

7.
✗	A **king's** life is different from a **Prime Minister**.
✓	A king's life is different from a **Prime Minister's**.
C	In a comparative statement of this kind, if the first noun is in the **possessive case**, the **second noun** too must be in the **possessive case**.

8.
✗	I gave him one and a half **rupee**.
✓	I gave him one and a half **rupees**.
C	Anything **greater than** one, even by a narrow margin, takes the **plural form**.

9.
✗	Has your brother bought a new **dress**?
✓	Has your brother bought a new **suit**?
C	A common error. Remember that whereas **men** and boys wear '**suits**', only **women** and girls wear '**dresses**'; though 'evening dress' is the general word for both sexes.

10. ✗ When I entered the compartment there was **no place** for me.

    ✓ When I entered the compartment there was **no room** for me.

    C In this sense the proper word is **room** which means an **unoccupied. seat or berth**.

11. ✗ When I entered the bedroom, I saw a snake crawling on the **ground**.

    ✓ When I entered the bedroom, I saw a snake crawling on the **floor**.

    C The **ground** is **part of the house**, whereas the **floor** constitutes **a part of the room**.

12. ✗ I get a monthly allowance of **hundred** rupees.

    ✓ I get a monthly allowance of a **hundred** rupees.

    C The word '**hundred**' must always be proceeded by the indefinite article 'a'.

13. ✗ Summarise the **two first** chapters of this book.

    ✓ Summarise the **first two** chapters of this book.

    C Obviously **there cannot be two first** chapters, just as there cannot be two last chapters.

14. ✗ He sold **three dozens** mangoes.

   ✓ He sold **three dozen** mangoes.

   C If '**dozen**' is preceded by a **numeral** (say, three, four, five, etc.) or by '**a**', use the **singular form**. The plural form is used in such sentences as 'We saw dozens of elephants, and hundreds of pigeons'.

15. ✗ I have just **taken** my meals.

   ✓ I have just had my food (or lunch, dinner).

   C Since we never have more than one meal at a time, why use the plural form? Besides, **use** the verb '**have**', not '**take**'.

16. ✗ I have finished **three-fourth** of this book.

   ✓ I have finished **three-fourths** of this book.

   C '**Three-fourths**' implies **three parts out of four** parts; therefore use the plural form.

PRONOUNS

1. ✗ He bought a radio for Rs. 250 and sold **the same** at a handsome profit.

| ✓ | He bought a radio for Rs. 250 and sold it at a handsome profit. |

| C | There is a common tendency to use this superfluous expression, '**the same**', where the pronoun '**it**' would be more suitable. Avoid writing 'I enclose a cheque for Rs. 175, please acknowledge receipt of the same'. |

2.
✗	My **sister and myself** are pleased to accept your invitation to dinner.
✓	My **sister and I** are pleased to accept your invitation to dinner.
C	Where no particular emphasis is intended, use the **simple pronouns 'he, you, I'**.

Note, for instance, 'I myself was to blame for the accident', or, reflexively, as 'The child hurt itself'.

3.
✗	The visitors **enjoyed** during their brief stay in Hyderabad.
✓	The visitors **enjoyed themselves** during their brief stay in Hyderabad.
C	'Enjoy' is a **transitive verb**, it **must** therefore be **acompanied by an object**, which may be a noun or a reflexive pronoun.

4.
| ✗ | I shall **avail** of this opportunity to meet you there. |
| ✓ | I shall **avail myself** of this opportunity to meet you there. |

	C	The **verb 'avail'** must here be **followed** by a **reflexive pronoun**.
5.	✗	My children cannot endure my **separation**.
	✓	My children cannot endure **separation** from me.
	C	It is not 'someone's separations but '**separation from someone**'.
6.	✗	May I now take **your leave**?
	✓	May I now take **leave of you**?
	C	To ask to be away from someone is not to take something which is in his possession.
7.	✗	Can you see me at **mine** tomorrow afternoon?
	✓	Can you see me at **my house** tomorrow afternoon?
	C	We can use 'mine', 'yours', etc. **only when** the word '**house**' has **already appeared in this context**. For instance, 'If you can't come to my house, I can meet you at yours'.
8.	✗	Will you lend me your pencil, please?— **Take**.
	✓	Will you lend me your pencils please?— **Take it**.

	C	In correct English usages the verb '**take**' must be **followed** by a suitable **noun** or **pronoun**.
9.	✗	**Whom** do you think will be dismissed first?
	✓	**Who**, do you think, will be dismissed first?
	C	If you ignore the parenthesis 'do you think', it should be easier to know why '**whom**' **is wrong**. 'Who will be dismissed first', not 'Whom.'
10.	✗	One should always remain loyal to **his** country.
	✓	One should always remain loyal to **one's** country.
	C	The indefinite pronoun 'one' must **always agree** with one of its parts: '**oneself**', '**one's**', '**one**', etc.
11.	✗	I request your favour of considering me for a transfer.
	✓	I request the favour of your considering me for a transfer.
	C	Another typical error—not '**your state of mind**', but '**the state of your mind**'.
12.	✗	You are fairer than **me**.
	✓	You are fairer than **I**.

	C	The complete sentence would read '**You are fairer than I am**'.
13.	✗	He is twenty years old, isn't **it**?
	✓	He is twenty years old, isn't **he**?
	C	In the second part of the sentence, the **object** of the **verb 'is'** is '**he**' not '**it**'.
14.	✗	Rita, having finished her paper, **she left** the examination hall.
	✓	Rita, having finished her paper, **left** the examination hall.
	C	This is an example of a **pronoun used where it** is **not required**.

ADJECTIVES

1.	✗	He has read almost **each** book of the college library.
	✓	He has read almost **every** book of the college library.
	C	***Each*** is a determiner which is used to refer to everyone of the two or more things and cannot be used with ***almost***.
2.	✗	**Every** one of the two pencils is missing.
	✓	**Each** one of the two pencils is missing.

> **C** 'Each' is used when each one (of two or more) is taken separately one by one. 'Every' is always used for more than two things, in a group or set. But both 'each and 'every' are invariably singular. e.g. 'Every (each) one of the nine apples was rotten.'

3. ✗ He is suffering from a **strong** cold.

   ✓ He is suffering from a **bad** cold.

   > **C** Also a 'bad headache', a 'bad stomach'.

4. ✗ You must secure at least **passable** marks.

   ✓ You must secure at least **pass** marks.

   > **C** The word **'passable'** has a different meaning—it **means 'tolerably good'**. For marks sufficient to pass an examination, we must say 'pass marks', not 'passing marks', which is however, another common error.

5. ✗ I am forty **years**.

   ✓ I am forty **years old**.

   > **C** **Either drop the word 'years'** and simply say 'I am forty', **or use the complete expression, 'I am forty**

years old', or 'I am forty years of age'.

6. ✗ He brought me milk, butter and honey, the **latter** being Indian.

   ✓ He brought me milk, butter and honey, the last being Indian.

   C **'Latter' is used only where two things are mentioned.**

7. ✗ This feat was **marvelous** well performed.

   ✓ This feat was **marvelously** well performed.

   C **Do not use an adjective to qualify an adverb.**

8. ✗ This car is superior **than** that.

   ✓ This car is superior **to that**.

   C Always **use** the **preposition 'to' after 'superior'** or **'inferior'**. Similarly say 'preferable to', not 'preferable than'.

VERBS

1. ✗ I **am living** in Bangalore.

   ✓ I **live** in Bangalore.

   C This is a typical Indianism. Why unnecessarily use the present participle when a **simple present tense can be more direct**?

2.
- ✗ She sang very well, **isn't it**?
- ✓ She sang very well, **didn't she**?
- C The expression 'isn't it?' is often used indiscriminately. In all such sentences, the tense and person used in the main statement must be retained in the auxiliary as well'. The auxiliary in this case 'didn't she' implies 'didn't she sing very well?

3.
- ✗ I **have read** an interesting book yesterday.
- ✓ I **read** an interesting book yesterday.
- C If the action was completed in the past at a particular time ('yesterday'), we should use the **simple past tense, not the present perfect**.

4.
- ✗ He **saw** the Taj at Agra.
- ✓ He **has seen** the Taj at Agra.
- C When the accent is more on the result of a past action than on the action itself, use the **present perfect tense**.

5.
- ✗ Sandeepa told me that she **may** proceed on leave.
- ✓ Sandeepa told me that she **might** proceed on leave.

> **C** A typical example of the wrong **use** of sequence of tenses. **Verbs in the subordinate** clauses **must** always **agree with the verb in the principal clause**. Similarly, say "I thought I could help him', not 'I thought I can help him'.

6. ✗ He walks as if the earth **belongs** to him.

   ✓ He walks as if the earth **belonged** to him.

   > **C** Expressions like 'as if', 'as though', are always **followed** by the **past tense**.

7. ✗ Kindly **see** my testimonials.

   ✓ Kindly **look at** (or examine) my testimonials.

   > **C** '**Seeing**' merely implies a **simple faculty** of **vision, devoid of any critical attention**. Isn't it possible to 'see' a thing, without 'looking at' it? Similarly, it is wrong to say 'I am seeing this great painting' (Right: 'I am looking at this great painting').

8. ✗ My sister always **puts on** a white saree.

   ✓ My sister always **wears** a white saree.

| | C | Whereas 'to put on' implies a **simple act**, **'to wear'** denotes **'putting on'** something **more habitually**. |

9.
- ✗ He **avenged** himself for the injustice done to his father.
- ✓ He revenged himself for the injustice done to his father.
- C The verbs '*avenged*' and '*revenged*' are often confused and misused. Whereas **'to revenge oneself' should be used for any wrong done to oneself, 'to avenge' means to inflict retribution (punishment) on behalf of somebody else**.

10.
- ✗ She **revenged** her father's murder.
- ✓ She **avenged** her father's murder.
- C As explained (9C).

11.
- ✗ I **slept rather** late last night.
- ✓ I **went to bed** rather late last night.
- C **'Going to bed'** implies a simple **act of getting into bed, for sleeping**. But it is possible that one may go to bed at ten, and not go to sleep until twelve o'clock.

12.
- ✗ He has **left** painting.
- ✓ He has **given up** painting.

> **C** It is **wrong** to use the **verb 'to leave'** in the sense of **'giving up' something**. 'Leave off' may be used, however.

13. ✗ **Leave** my arm, please.

    ✓ **Let go** my arm, please.

    > **C** The **verb 'leave' cannot be** used in sense of **'giving up one's hold'**.

14. ✗ He asked me **where was** I going.

    ✓ He asked me **where I was** going.

    > **C** Once a statement is made in the reported speech ('he asked where..'), it is **wrong to retain the question form** ('where was I going?').

15. ✗ I should feel happy if you **will** come to tea tomorrow.

    ✓ I should feel happy if you **would** come to tea tomorrow.

    > **C** **Verbs in both these clauses should agree with each other**, e.g., should, would, not should, will. Even if the first sentence is permissible, still it is a less polite form of saying the same thing.

16. ✗ I should like **to forward** myself as a candidate for this post.

    ✓ I should like **to offer** myself as a candidate for this post.

	C	**Forward** means **to send on** or **to dispatch an object**. How can, therefore, one 'forward' oneself?
17.	✗	Hundreds of people **died** by the earthquake.
	✓	Hundreds of people were **killed** by the earthquake.
	C	We **'die' of natural causes** ('illness', 'heart-failure', etc.), but **in the case of unexpected calamities** ('fire', 'war', etc.) we must **use the verb 'kill'**.
18.	✗	Will you kindly **open** this knot?
	✓	Will you kindly **untie** this knot?
	C	A very common error. One **'opens'** a door or a window, **but not a 'knot'**.
19.	✗	I have to **give** another examination next year.
	✓	I have to **take** another examination next year.
	C	An **examiner gives** an examination or a test, a **candidate takes** an examination or a test.
20.	✗	Where have you **kept** the pencil I gave you a few minutes ago?
	✓	Where have you **put** (placed) the pencil I gave you a few minutes ago?

> **C** The verb '**to keep**' implies a **certain duration**, e.g., 'He always keeps his diaries under lock and key'. But '**putting**' something implies '**placing**' it temporarily somewhere.

21. **✗** **Better revise** this essay.

    ✓ You **had better** revise this essay.

    C The **correct structural pattern** is 'You had better do this first', 'You had better sleep now', etc.

22. **✗** Don't hold this dirty insect in your hand; **throw it**.

    ✓ Don't hold this dirty insect in your hand; **throw it away**.

    C '**To throw something away**' is the **correct** (and complete) expression. 'To throw' means 'to throw a ball', etc. 'To throw something away' means 'to throw it aside'.

23. **✗** It is better to keep one's head in the face of danger than **losing** one's courage and getting panicky.

    ✓ It is better to keep one's head in the face of danger than **to lose** one's courage and get panicky.

    C A case of confusion of verbs; one form of verb should not be mixed with another form of verb in this way—**if the first verb is in the infinitive**

mood, the second verb should also be in the infinitive mood.

24. ✗ Are you a vegetarian? **Yes**, I am not.

✓ Are you a vegetarian? **No**, I am not. (Or, Yes, I am.)

C **When the answer is in the affirmative, say 'Yes'** and drop the negative form 'not'. **If the answer is in the negative, say 'No'**, and you, may also retain the negative '**not**'.

25. ✗ When he lost my book I **became** very angry.

✓ When he lost my book I **felt** very angry

C It is better to use '**feel**' or '**get**' with **adjectives** such as '**angry**', '**hungry**', '**thirsty**', '**tired**', etc.

26. ✗ I went to London with a view **to investigate** the matter.

✓ I went to London with a view **to investigating** the matter.

C '**With a view to**' is **always followed by a gerund** and not an infinitive.

27. ✗ I did nothing but **cried**.

✓ I did nothing but **cry**.

C **Use the infinitive after 'but'.**

28.
- ✗ Will you kindly **mend** this pencil?
- ✓ Will you kindly **sharpen** this pencil?'
- C **One 'sharpens' a pencil**, but '**mends**' a pen.

29.
- ✗ I want you to **fully realise** the consequences of this.
- ✓ I want you to **realise fully** the consequences of this.
- C **Avoid the use of split infinitive.** Don't insert anything between the words 'to feel', 'to remember', etc.

30.
- ✗ The **thief escaped** before I opened the door.
- ✓ The thief had escaped before I opened the door.
- C The **earlier action** should **always take the past perfect verb**.

31.
- ✗ Rita and I **was walking** in the garden.
- ✓ Rita and I **were walking** in the garden.
- C The verb has to be in plural when the subject of the sentence Rita and I is plural.

32.
- ✗ The whole class **were playing**.

✓	The whole class **was** playing.
C	The whole class indicates a single entity.

33.
✗	Both of us **was present** at the bus stop.
✓	Both of us **were present** at the bus stop.
C	The verb has to be in plural because ***both of us*** is a plural expression.

34.
✗	All my books **is** with her.
✓	All my books **are** with her.
C	'All my books', the subject of the sentence, is **plural**.

35.
✗	Each one of these apples **are** red.
✓	Each one of these apples **is** red.
C	***Each one*** suggests that the subject is singular; it does not refer to all members of the set.

36.
✗	A grey and a white dog **is** barking.
✓	A grey and a white dog **are** barking.
C	There are two entities as the subject (i.e. ***a grey dog*** and ***a white dog***), so the verb is plural).

37.
✗	My brother and my sister is at the party

✓	My brother and my sister are at the party.
C	The verb is plural because the subject (i.e. *my brother* and *my sister* is plural).

38.
✗	She and I **was** drinking milk.
✓	She and I **were** drinking milk.
C	The verb is plural because the subject (i.e. *she* and *I* is plural).

39.
✗	Slow and steady **win** the race.
✓	Slow and steady **wins** the race.
C	The understood subject (person) is singular, so the verb is singular.

40.
✗	Tomorrow never **come**.
✓	Tomorrow never **comes**.
C	'*Tomorrow* the subject of the sentence is' singular.

41.
✗	Neither red nor black **suit** me.
✓	Neither red nor black **suits** me.
C	The understood subject (e.g. *cloth*) is singular.

42.
✗	Either Rita or Natasha **have** eaten the ice cream.
✓	Either Rita or Natasha **has** eaten the ice cream.

	C	When an exclusive coordinator (e.g *either or*) is used the verb agrees with its nearest subject (i.e. *Natasha*).
43.	**✗**	Neither my father nor my mother **are** going to the party.
	✓	Neither my father nor my mother is going to the party.
	C	The exclusive coordinator makes the verb agree with its nearest subject (i.e. *my mother*) which is singular.
44.	**✗**	The President as well as the Prime Minister **is** in the plane.
	✓	The President as well as the Prime Minister **are** in the plane.
	C	*As well as* is like *and*; because of it, the subject of the sentence is plural and needs a plural verb.
45.	**✗**	Either the whole class or I **are** in the wrong.
	✓	Either the whole class or I **am** in the wrong.
	C	In sentences with exclusive coordinators (i. e. *either... or*), the verb agrees with its nearest subject.
46.	**✗**	The news, which you have given me, **are** excellent.
	✓	The news, which you have given me, **is** excellent.

	C	***News*** is an uncountable noun and is singular.
47.	✗	Alms **were** asked by the poor.
	✓	Alms **was** asked by the poor.
	C	***Alms***, the subject of the sentence, is a singular noun and needs a singular verb.
48.	✗	My friend and guide, my teacher **were** alive, when I decided to join the army.
	✓	My friend and guide, my teacher **was** alive, when I decided to join the army.
	C	The subject of this sentence (i.e. ***my teacher***) is singular, ***My friend and guide*** are attributes of the subject.
49.	✗	None of the boys **were** wearing a cap.
	✓	None of the boys **was** wearing a cap.
	C	The subject of the sentence (i.e. ***none of the boys***) is singular. ***None*** means ***not any (one)***.
50.	✗	Neither Mr Robin nor his colleagues **is** going for the vacation.
	✓	Neither Mr Robin nor his colleagues **are** going for the vacation.
	C	Because of the exclusive coordinator neither nor, the verb agrees with its nearest subject (i.e. ***his colleagues***).

51. ✗ My spectacles **has** been stolen.
    ✓ My spectacles **have** been stolen.
    C *Spectacles* is a plural noun and needs a plural verb.

52. ✗ My trousers **was** black in colour.
    ✓ My trousers **were** black in colour.
    C *Trousers* is a plural subject and needs a plural verb.

53. ✗ **Was** there many girls present for the meeting?
    ✓ **Were** there many girls present for the meeting?
    C *Many girls*, the plural subject, needs a plural verb.

54. ✗ Each of these umbrellas **are** defective.
    ✓ Each of these umbrellas **is** defective.
    C The subject of the sentence, *each* needs a singular verb.

55. ✗ The teachers as well as the students **was** surprised.
    ✓ The teachers as well as the students **were** surprised.
    C As well as is like and the verb agrees with the whole expression that is

the subject of the sentence (i.e. ***the teacher as well as the students***).

ADVERBS

1. ✗ "Isn't he the best player in the Hockey Eleven?"–."**Of cours**e, he is".

   ✓ Isn't he the best player in the Hockey Eleven?– "**Certainly**, he is".

   C '**Of course**' should be **used** only in the **context of an inevitable consequence**.

2. ✗ He bore **cheerfully his miseries**.

   ✓ He bore his **miseries cheerfully**.

   C In the case of a transitive verb, **use the adverb after the object**.

3. ✗ He is too **polite**.

   ✓ He is too **polite to be unkind** to anyone.

   C '**He is too polite' is incomplete**. 'Too polite' for what? *Too* means 'excessively', 'to a higher degree than is desirable'.

4. ✗ The spectators left the theatre **by and by**.

   ✓ The spectators left the theatre **one by one**.

	C	**'By and by'** means 'eventually', and not 'one by one'.
5.	✗	I shall be back **just now**.
	✓	I shall be back **presently**.
	C	***Just now*** means 'at the present time' whereas ***'presently'*** means 'after a short time' or 'soon'.
6.	✗	This morning I got up **lately**.
	✓	This morning I got up **late**.
	C	**'Lately' is not the opposite of 'early'** ('early' has the opposite 'late'). 'Lately' means 'not long ago', 'recently'.
7.	✗	I **never met** him today.
	✓	I **did not meet** him today.
	C	**'Never' means 'not ever'**, except when used for very strong emphasis.

PREPOSITIONS

1.	✗	Please write your names **with** ink.
	✓	Please write your names **in** ink.
	C	Always say **'write in chalk'**, **'write in pencil'**, etc., but **'write with a pen'**.
2.	✗	He caught the thief **from** the hand.
	✓	He caught the thief **by** the hand.

	C	Similarly, say 'seize, hold, or **take by the hand**'.
3.	✗	He is sitting **on** his table.
	✓	He is sitting **at** his table.
	C	Also, '**sit at a piano**', '**sit at one's desk**', but '**sit on a bench**', '**sit on a sofa**'.
4.	✗	Why do you now repent **from** your misdeeds?
	✓	Why do you now repent **of** your misdeeds?
	C	***Repent*** of (something) is an idiomatic expression; i.e. only *of* is used in this context.
5.	✗	The Principal **disposed** the application in no time.
	✓	The Principal **disposed** of the application in no time.
	C	Don't forget to **say 'dispose of'**, '**accuse of**', '**distrust of**', '**dislike of**', '**repent of**' etc.
6.	✗	You are preventing me **to** leave the room.
	✓	You are preventing me **from** leaving the room.
	C	Other words followed by '**from**' **are** '**release**', '**prohibit**', '**exempt.**'

7.
- ✗ I live **at** Delhi.
- ✓ I live **in** Delhi.
- C Use **'at' for small places** and 'in' **for large cities**.

8.
- ✗ I went to Madras **for** attending a meeting.
- ✓ I went to Madras **to** attend a meeting. Or, I went to Madras **for** a meeting.
- C After **verbs of motion**, purpose can be shown by
  (i) **'to' and an infinitive**, or
  (ii) **'for' and a noun or pronoun**.

9.
- ✗ He was debarred **to** sit for the I.A.S. examination.
- ✓ He was debarred **from** sitting for the I.A.S. examination.
- C One is always debarred from doing something.

10.
- ✗ He went **with** the bus.
- ✓ He went **by** bus.
- C Always say **'by taxi', 'by air', 'by land', 'by train', 'by boat', 'by tonga'**, but **'on foot', 'on horseback'**.

11.
- ✗ This book comprises **of five** sections.
- ✓ This book comprises **five** sections.

C	A very common mistake. **Don't use any preposition after 'comprise'**. You may say 'This book consists of five sections'.
12. ✗	Let me congratulate you **for** your son's marriage.
✓	Let me congratulate you **on** your son's marriage.
C	We always *congratulate* someone **on** something, it is a fixed collocation.
13. ✗	He died **from** cholera.
✓	He died **of** cholera.
C	A person, animal or plant always dies *of* something; it is a fixed collocation.
14. ✗	Ram's pen is different **than** his brother's.
✓	Ram's pen is different **from** his brother's.
C	With *different* we always use the preposition *from*.
15. ✗	He is good **in** English.
✓	He is good **at** English.
C	Similarly, **'clever at'**, **'poor at'**, **'quick at'**, **'slow at'** etc.

16.
- ✗ Natasha is married **with** a rich banker.
- ✓ Natasha is married **to** a rich banker.
- C A man is married *to* a woman; it is a fixed collocation.

17.
- ✗ I have been **searching** my pen since morning.
- ✓ I have been **searching for** my pen since morning.
- C **Without the preposition 'for', 'to search' will mean 'to look into', 'to examine'.**

   For instance, 'The customs officer searched his suitcases', 'The police inspector searched his house'.

18.
- ✗ I don't **wish** any compensation.
- ✓ I don't **wish** for any compensation.
- C One always *wishes for* something.

19.
- ✗ Who will buy this car **for** such a price?
- ✓ Who will buy this car **at** such a price?
- C **Use 'for' only where a specific amount is mentioned.** e.g., 'He sold his Guitar for Rs. 500'.

20.
- ✗ I shall return this book **after** a week.
- ✓ I shall return this book **in** a week (or, in a week's time).
- C In this sense '**in**' means '**at the end of**'.

21.
- ✗ He took **out** his shoes before entering the mosque.
- ✓ He took off his shoes before entering the mosque.
- C *To take something out* means '*to destroy, or disable something*'. Whereas *to take something off* means '**to remove from one's body**'. These plural verbs have other meanings as well.

22.
- ✗ The train is running **in** time.
- ✓ The train is running **on** time.
- C 'On time' means '**punctual**' whereas *in* time means '**eventually**' or '**not late**'.

23.
- ✗ He has lost the match **from** his rival.
- ✓ He has lost the match **to** his rival.
- C One always *loses* something *to* someone.

24.
- ✗ Where have you **been to**?

- ✓ Where have you **been**?
- C The question is about one's location and not movement which *to* suggests.

25.
- ✗ Open the **seventh page** of this book.
- ✓ Open this book at **page seven**.
- C *At* suggests location rather than space which *open* suggests.

CONJUNCTIONS

1.
- ✗ Kiran, as well as Kamal, are leaving for England.
- ✓ Kiran, as well as Kamal, **is** leaving for England.
- C When **two singular nouns** are **linked by 'as well as'**, they **take a singular verb**.

2.
- ✗ Unless you **do not work** hard, you will not succeed.
- ✓ Unless you **work** hard, you will not succeed.
- C **Note** that **'unless' means 'if not'**, therefore you **cannot use a double negative**.

3.
- ✗ **Until** you remain restless you cannot concentrate.

✓	**So long as** you remain restless you cannot concentrate.
C	**You cannot use a double negative.**

4.
✗	Literature has no other aim **but** entertainment.
✓	Literature has no other aim **than** entertainment.
C	The correct usage is '**other than**', **not 'other but'**.

5.
✗	The book contains **five hundred fifty pages**.
✓	The book contains **five hundred and fifty pages**.
C	It is a convention in English to add ***and*** between hundred and the last digit(s).

6.
✗	An old teacher is **as if** the father of his pupils.
✓	An old teacher is, **as it were**, the father of his pupils.
C	***As if*** means "as would be the case if" whereas ***as it were*** means 'in a way'.

7.
✗	I am going to Delhi **because** I may see my aunt.
✓	I am going to Delhi **in order** that I may see my aunt.

Or, I am going to Delhi to see my aunt.

C — **'Because' implies some reason or cause**; it should not, therefore, be used to express purpose.

8. ✗ He **asked that where** I lived.

✓ He **asked where I** lived.

C — *That* is not needed if a clause that begins with a *wh*-word is added to the main clause as its complement.

ARTICLES

1. ✗ We shall see him **after the** dinner.

✓ We shall see him **after** dinner.

C — There is often a tendency to use the definite article 'the' where it is not required. **Remember that the definite article is not used before the names of the meals 'supper', 'dinner', 'lunch', 'breakfast'.**

2. ✗ Does your sister go **to the** school?

✓ Does your sister go **to** school?

C — **'Goes to the school' means to visit a particular school, whereas 'to go to school' means to go to school customarily as a teacher or a pupil.** Similarly it would be wrong to say 'I go to the mosque every Friday', when the correct expression is 'I go to mosque every Friday'. The latter sentence means 'to go and pray', while the former sentence means 'to go and visit the mosque'.

3. ✗ What kind **of a** friend are you?

   ✓ What kind **of** friend are you?

   C **Don't use 'a' or 'an'** (the indefinite article) **after the phrase 'sort of' or 'kind of'**.

4. ✗ Cholera has broken out in the **whole** Nagpur.

   ✓ Cholera has broken out in the **whole of** Nagpur.

   C **Don't use 'the whole' with proper nouns**; say 'the whole of India', not 'the whole India'.

5. ✗ I have **headache**.

   ✓ I have a **headache**.

   C Note the following phrases which involve the use of the indefinite article, 'a sore throat', 'a bad cold', 'a severe pain', 'on a large scale', 'on an average', 'at a loss', 'as a rule', etc.

6. ✗ There are **many a books** you can choose from.

| ✓ | There is **many a book** you can choose from. |

| C | **'Many a book' takes a singular verb**, although it is equivalent in sense to 'many books'. This phrase is now rather old-fashioned. |

7. | ✗ | Every Sunday evening we go to **theatre**. |

| ✓ | Every Sunday evening we go to **the theatre**. |

| C | **One must use the definite article before 'concert', 'cinema', 'circus', 'show' etc.** |

8. | ✗ | **Aeroplane** has conquered time and space. |

| ✓ | **The aeroplane** has conquered time and space. |

| C | **Here 'the aeroplane' stands for the aeroplane as a category**; it is a generic use. Similarly, the owl, the dog, the radio, the taperecorder, etc. stand for different groups of entities. |

9. | ✗ | One must learn to distinguish **good** from bad. |

| ✓ | One must learn to distinguish **the good** from the bad. |

| C | When **adjectives** are **used as nouns**

to mean a whole class of things or persons, we **must use** the **definite article**.

10.
- ✗ Don't make **noise**.
- ✓ Don't make **a noise**.
- C Similarly, say 'make an effort', 'make a mistake'.

11.
- ✗ I am certain that he is **in right**.
- ✓ I am certain that he is **in the right**.
- C The correct phrases are **'in the wrong'**, **'in the right'**, **'in the negative'**, **'in the positive'**.

12.
- ✗ Is this an Oxford or Cambridge publication?
- ✓ Is this an Oxford or a Cambridge publication?
- C This refers to two entities, one of them (Oxford) begins with a vowel and the other a consonant sound.

MISCELLANEOUS

1.
- ✗ **What to** speak of English, he cannot even talk in Hindustani.
- ✓ He cannot even talk in Hindustani, **not to** speak of English.

2. ✗ What **to do**?

   ✓ What can **be done**?

   Or, What's **to be done**?

   Or, What shall **we do**? **What are we to do**?

   C Between *what* and the infinite *to do* we need a finite verb (e.g) *is*.

3. ✗ The old widower could not make **his both ends** meet.

   ✓ The old widower could not make **both ends** meet.

   C No insertion is permitted in a *frozen* idiom.

4. ✗ I enquired **of** his health.

   ✓ I enquired **about (or after)** his health.

   C We *enquire about* something or *of* someone. To *enquire after* means to ask about someone's health or wellbeing.

5. ✗ I spoke to him **with** a lower tone.

   ✓ I spoke to him **in** a lower tone.

   C In a *lower tone* means *in a tone* containing a lower pitch.

6. ✗ This custom has come down since **times** immemorial.

	✓	This custom has come down since **time** immemorial.
	C	We use *since* when we have one stretch of time.
7.	✗	To laugh **or weep** is entirely our own choice.
	✓	To laugh **or to** weep is entirely our own choice.
	C	**When 'and' or 'or' link two dissimilar notions, 'to' must be inserted.**
8.	✗	I don't remember **him ever** helping me.
	✓	I don't remember **his ever** helping me.
	C	When the verb is in the participate form, the subject assumes a possessive form.
9.	✗	I can't allow you to **cut** jokes in the class.
	✓	I can't allow you to **make** jokes in the class.
	C	**We 'make' jokes**, not 'cut' them. '*To make* means to cause something to come about; the idiom *crack a joke* refers to a critical joke.

10. ✗ He never has, and **never** will permit such practices in his office.

    ✓ He never has permitted **nor ever** will permit such practices in his office.

    C **Both verbs 'has permitted' and 'will permit' must be used in their complete forms**.

11. ✗ He has no **issues**.

    ✓ He has no **issue**.

    C In the sense of '**offspring**' the word '**issue**' should not be used in the plural form.

12. ✗ **His both hands** have been injured.

    ✓ **Both of his hands** have been injured.

    C In *both of his hands* both is like a pronoun in *both his parents* both is a predetermined which precedes that determines *his*.

13. ✗ Why **not we** send words to him immediately?

    ✓ Why **don't we** send word to him immediately?

    C We cannot use *not* without its being preceded by an auxiliary verb. If no such verb exists, an appropriate form of do is used.

14. ✗ There are **many worth seeing places** in Agra.

   ✓ There are many **places worth seeing** in Agra.

   C In English, the relative clause e.g. which is *worth-seeing* or its reduced form is put after that noun to which it is attached.

15. ✗ He said to me **if you like you may go**.

   ✓ He told me that if **I liked I might go**.

   C In a hypothetical situation in the past, both the conditional clause and the consequent clause will have the past tense form.

16. ✗ I don't know **who** I can trust.

   ✓ I don't know **whom** I can trust.

   C As who is the object to the verb *trust*, its usual form is *whom*. However, in modern English, who is also used.

SOME MORE ERRORS

With Nouns and Noun-Phrases

1. ✗ We have received no **informations**.
   ✓ We have received no **information**.
   C *Information* is never used in plural.

2. ✗ He told **these news** to his mother.
   ✓ He told his mother **this news**, *or* He **told *this*** news to his mother.
   ✓ Since *news* is singular, it cannot have a plural determiner (i.e. *these*).

3. ✗ I packed my **luggages**.
   ✓ I packed my **luggage**.
   C The noun *luggage* does not have a plural form.

4. ✗ The sceneries here **are** not good.
   ✓ The scenery here **is** not good.
   C The word *scenery* is an uncountable noun and has no plural.

5. ✗ I have lost my **furnitures**.
   ✓ I have lost my **furniture**.
   C *Furniture* is an uncountable (mass) noun and has no plural.

6.
- ✗ There **are** no **breads** in this shop.
- ✓ There is no **bread** in this shop.
- ✓ There are no **loaves** in this shop.
- C *Bread* is an uncountable noun and has no plural form.

7.
- ✗ Please excuse **the troubles**.
- ✓ Please excuse **me for the trouble** (I have caused).
- C *Trouble* is an uncountable (mass) noun and has no plural.

8.
- ✗ He took **troubles to do** his work.
- ✓ He took **pains over** his work.
- ✓ He took **trouble over** his work.
- C *Trouble* is a mass noun.

9.
- ✗ In some parts of the world there are many **poors**.
- ✓ In some parts of the world there are many **poor people**.
- C *Poor* as a noun is a collective noun and means the *poor people*.

10.
- ✗ Scouts wear **half pants**.
- ✗ Students should wear **white pants**.
- ✓ Scouts wear **shorts**.
- ✓ Student; should wear **white trousers**.

| C | In British English *pants* means 'underpants' or '*knickers*'; in American English they mean trousers. *Half pants* is an Indian English expression for *shorts* in British English. In American English, *shorts* are 'underpants'. |

11.
✗	I spent the holidays with my **family members**.
✓	I spent the holidays with **the members of my family**.
✓	I spent the holidays with **my family**.
C	Since *family* means 'a group of people related by blood or marriage', *family member* is a redundant expression.

12.
✗	There is **no place** in this compartment.
✓	There is **no room** in this compartment.
C	*Place* refers to a location whereas room refers to a space that can be occupied.

13.
| ✗ | Write this in your **copy**. |
| ✓ | Write this in your **notebook**. |
| C | As a noun copy means a single specimen of a particular book or document whereas a ***copybook*** means

a book containing models of hand writing to be learnt.

14.
- ✗ I am learning a new **poetry**.
- ✓ I am learning a new **poem**.
- C When we refer to **poetry**, we refer to **the entire genre** and not to a particular work of a poet.

15.
- ✗ We saw a **joker** at the circus.
- ✓ We saw a **clown** at the circus.
- C **Clown** is a **comic entertainer especially one in a circus**, whereas a 'joker' is **a person who is foolish or inept**. Therefore, it is appropriate to use *clown* in this context.

16.
- ✗ We had a good **play** of football.
- ✓ We had a good **game** of football.
- C 'Play' is generally **used** as a **verb** and **game** is used is a **noun it means 'sport played'** according to **rules**.

17.
- ✗ We saw a **theatre**.
- ✓ We saw a **play**.
- C **A theatre is a building in which plays are enacted**, not the play itself.

18.
- ✗ The boy was wearing a **new dress**.

	✓	The boy was wearing a **new suit** (some new clothes).
	C	**Dress** is generally used with **reference to a woman's attire**, but we do say 'a man in full dress' or 'evening dress'.
19.	✗	Please put your sign here.
	✓	Please put your **signature** here.
	C	In a sentence where the term 'sign' means 'to write one's name', it is a verb. '**Signature**' on the other hand **is a noun, which means 'the act of writing.**" 'Sign' when used as a noun, means 'a symbol'.
20.	✗	He is my **cousin brother**.
	✓	He is my **cousin**.
	C	The English language uses much more loosely terms expressing relationship than the Indian languages. 'Aunt' means the sister of either father or mother, 'Uncle' means the brother of either father or mother '**Cousin' means any child of any aunt or uncle**.
21.	✗	He had a large **number** of money.
	✓	He had a large **amount** of money.
	C	Money is an uncountable (mass) noun.

22.
- ✗ Some of my **servant tells** me.
- ✓ Some of my **servants tell** me.
- C *Some* means at least more than one and needs a plural verb.

23.
- ✗ The front/back **side of** the house.
- ✓ The front/back **of** the house.
- C The terms '*front*' and '*back*' refer to different sides; the word *side*' is redundant here.

24.
- ✗ I have hurt a **foot**-finger.
- ✓ I have hurt a **toe**.
- C The five digits at the end of the human foot are called *toe's*, and not foot fingers.

25.
- ✗ He is a tall **gentleman**.
- ✓ He is a tall **man**.
- C **'Gentleman' is a difficult word to use correctly in colloquial English**. Use 'gentleman' when they are referring to a man's character (he is a real gentleman e.g.', while praising him; he is not a gentleman, while criticizing him), and to use 'man' to denote an adult of the male sex.

26.
- ✗ I saw two **females**.

	✓	I saw two **women**.
	C	Similarly, don't be self-conscious over the use of 'lady' and 'woman'. The latter is the usual word and is quite polite. 'She is a lady' means that she is a woman of particularly good birth, breeding and taste.
27.	✗	He took **insult** at this.
	✓	He took **offence** at this.
	C	***Offence*** means 'annoyance' or resentment brought about by a perceived insult. Hence is the expression ***take offence***.
28.	✗	The box contains pens, papers and **others**.
	✓	The box contains pens, papers and **such things**.
	C	***Other*** as a pronoun is used to refer to things different from which is already mentioned. ***Such things*** refer to similar things.
29.	✗	In India there are many **poors**.
	✓	In India there are many poor (**people**).
	C	When the adjective ***poor*** is used in place of a noun, it has no plural form.
30.	✗	He provided the **blinds** with food.

	✓	He provided the **blind** with food.
	C	When the adjective ***blind*** is used as a noun, it does not have a plural form.
31.	✗	He bought a pair of half **hose**.
	✓	He bought a pair of **socks**.
	C	The term ***half hose*** is not used in modern English.
32.	✗	Give him some **blotting**.
	✓	Give him some **blotting paper**.
	C	***Blotting*** is the present participle of the verb ***blot*** which means to dry (a wet surface) using an absorbent material, e.g., a ***blotting*** paper.
33.	✗	Our **boarding** is full.
	✓	Our **boarding house** is full. Our hostel is full.
	C	***Boarding*** refers to an arrangement according to which pupils live in school during the term whereas a ***boarding*** house refers to a private house providing food and lodging to its paying guests.
34.	✗	Give my **B.C.s** to all.
	✓	Give my **kind (est) regards** to all.
	C	Avoid using short terms not in use.
35.	✗	He hit an **over boundary**.

	✓	He hit a **six or a sixer**.
	C	If a batsman hits for six runs, it is called a *sixer*, and not *over boundary*.
36.	✗	There are two **waiting members in our party**.
	✓	There are two **reserves on our side**.
	✓	There are two **reserves in our team**.
	C	Since we have a specific term *'reserve'* to refer to the waiting members of a team we call them by it.
37.	✗	We like **taking part** in drama.
	✓	We like **acting (plays)**.
	C	**'Drama' is rarely used nowadays in the sense in which an Indian schoolboy is likely to use it**, that is to say to mean a play, whether acted by professionals or amateurs.
38.	✗	We are all **fellow brothers**.
	✓	We are all **brothers**.
	C	As an adjective, the term *fellow* is redundant here because it refers to the sharing of a quality or relationship, which ***brothers*** indicates.
39.	✗	I passed the **noon** in study.

	✓	I spent the **middle of the day** working.
	C	'Noon' means exactly twelve o'clock in the middle of the day and not a period of time round about that hour.
40.	✗	He got a bad **companionship**.
	✓	He got into bad **company**.
	C	Note the difference between companionship & company.
41.	✗	One of my **servant** tells me.
	✓	One of my **servants** tells me.
	C	**The noun following 'one of', 'none of'; 'some of' and similar expressions must be plural in number**, with the verb should agree in number with the subject of the sentence, which is singular.
42.	✗	I **took a bath** in the sea.
	✓	I **had a bathe** in the sea.
	C	Use **'bath'** when the **object of entering the water is to clean yourself;** use **'bathe'** when the **object is to swim or to enjoy yourself**.

WITH PRONOUNS

1. ✗ Both **did not go**.
   ✓ Neither **went**.
   C If *both* are excluded from an action, we use *neither*.

2. ✗ Each of these boys **play** games.
   ✓ Each of these boys **plays** games.
   C The subject of the sentence, *each* is singular.

3. ✗ We all **did not** go.
   ✓ None of us **went**.
   C If *all* are excluded from an action, we use none.

4. ✗ One should not waste **his** time.
   ✓ A **man/boy** should not waste his time.
   ✓ One should not waste **one's** time.
   C If *one* is the subject of the sentence the genitive for it is one's.

5. ✗ "Have you a pen?" "I have not **got**."
   ✓ "Have you a pen?" "I have not got **one** or I **don't have** one."
   C *Have* is a transitive verb and needs an object to complete this sentence. The

referential expression for an object is ***it*** or one.

6.
- ✗ "Is he coming?" "Yes, **I think**."
- ✓ "Is he coming?" "Yes, **I think so**."
- C The pronominal expression for a statement is *so*; and not *it*. *Think* needs a sentence as its complement; so does the job.

7.
- ✗ He enjoyed during the **holidays**.
- ✓ He **enjoyed himself during** the holidays.
- C *Enjoy* means take to *pleasure* in an activity whereas *enjoy oneself* means ***have a pleasant time***.

8.
- ✗ The boy who does best **he will get** a prize.
- ✗ Whoever does best **he will get** a prize.
- ✓ The boy who does best will get a prize.
- ✓ Whoever does best will get a prize.
- C As the verb phrase ***will get a prize*** has already got a subject (e.g.) *the boy who does best* or ***whoever does best***, it does not need another subject.

9. ✗ "Who did this?" **"Myself."**
   ✓ "Who did this?" **"I (myself)."**
   C In response to the question, we have to use the subject of the sentence, i.e., I in this context *myself* can follow it for emphasis.

10. ✗ **I and he** are brothers.
    ✓ **He and I** are brothers.
    C **It is considered conceited to put 'I' first when there are two subjects.**

11. ✗ Jack **with some friends** went for a walk.
    ✓ Jack **went for a walk with some friends**.
    ✓ **Jack, along with his friends, went for a walk**.
    C The subject of the sentence is *Jack*. The companions can be mentioned at the end of the sentence by using *with*, or with the subject by using *along with*, separating it from the subject by commas.

12. ✗ She is wiser than **me**.
    ✓ She is wiser than **I**.
    C In traditional grammar *I* is preferred because the comparison is with than

I am. However, in spoken English, *I* is rarely used in British or American English.

13. ✗ Everyone is frightened when **they see** a tiger.

    ✓ Everyone is frightened when **he sees** a tiger.

    C **'Every' is a singular word**, which when attached to a singular man like *'one'* refers to all individual members of a group. **So, it will take a singular pronoun**.

14. ✗ None of us **have** seen him.

    ✓ None of us **has** seen him.

    C **'None' is a singular word**, therefore it will take a **singular verb**.

15. ✗ My books are better **than my friend**.

    ✓ My books are better **than those of my friend**.

    C When **comparing two things** in a sentence, **use 'that of', 'these of', 'those of'**.

16. ✗ One should work hard.

    ✓ **A man/boy** should work hard.

| | C | ***One*** is used to refer to the speaker or any person in general and should be avoided in specific contexts. |

17.
	✗	Here is my cup; please **fill**.
	✓	Here is my cup; please **fill it**.
	C	**All transitive verbs, including 'fill', must have an object**.

18.
	✗	I asked for my pencil, but he did not give **me**.
	✓	I asked for my pencil, but he did not give **it to me**.
	C	Some transitive verbs, e.g., '**give**' and '**lend**', **must have two objects to have a complete sentence**.

19.
	✗	The master tested the **boy if** he could read English.
	✓	The master tested whether the boy could read English.
	C	**The object of 'tested' is not 'boy' but the whole beginning with *whether* clause**.

20.
| | ✗ | I shall see the brakes **whether they** work well. |
| | ✓ | I shall see **whether the** brakes work well. |

21. **✗** People **starves** when he has no money.

    ✓ People **starve** when they have no money.

    C Note that 'every', 'none', 'much', 'person' are singular words; **'all', 'some', 'most', 'many' and 'people' are plural**. It is a very common mistake to use pronouns and possessive adjectives in the wrong number referring to any of the above-mentioned words.

22. **✗** The size of the shoe should be the same **as this** shoe.

    ✓ The size of the shoe should be the same **as that of this** shoe.

    C **In such comparative sentences** we must be careful to **compare the same part of two things**. 'That of', 'these of' and 'those of' are necessary words often omitted. 'His teaching was like Buddha 'is a very common mistake; 'that of Buddha' *must* be written.

WITH ADJECTIVES

1. **✗** **These all** mangoes are ripe.

| ✓ | **All these** mangoes are ripe. |
| C | A predetermines (e.g. **all**) precedes a determines (e.g. **these**) in English. |

2.
✗	I have no **any friends**.
✓	I have no **friends**.
C	As **no** means **not any**, we cannot use **no any**.

3.
✗	**Both** men **have** not come.
✓	**Neither** man **has** come.
C	When **both** is negated it becomes **neither**.

4.
✗	Open your book at six **page**.
✓	Open your book at **page six**.
C	A cardinal number (e.g. **six**) will always follow the noun (e.g. **page**) whereas an ordinal number (e.g. **sixth**) will always precede it (e.g. **sixth page**).

5.
✗	He is **elder** than I.
✓	He is **older** than I.
C	Though **elder** means **older**, it is used only when comparing two related people good.

6.
| ✗ | He is **more better** than I. |
| ✓ | He is **better** than 1. |

	C	Better itself in the comparative form for good.
7.	✗	He is **worst** than I.
	✓	He is **worse** than I.
	C	'**Worst**' is a superlative adjective for 'bad'. It cannot be used in a sentence where a comparison is made between two people.
8.	✗	He gets a **less** salary.
	✓	He gets a **small** salary.
	C	*Less* is a comparative form of *little*; it cannot be used when no comparison is made.
9.	✗	In our library the number of books *is less*.
	✓	In our library the number of books *is small*.
	C	No comparison is involved here.
10.	✗	Of the two plans this is the **best**.
	✓	Of the two plans this is the **better**.
	C	Best is the superlative form of *good*. While comparing two entities, we use **better**.
11.	✗	He is becoming **strong**.
	✓	He is becoming **stronger**.

C — **'He is becoming strong' is correct English.** However the comparative form can be used, when growth or change is implied in a sentence, or when the words 'than before' can be understood, e.g., talking of a boy's progress in class you can say, 'he is working well now', but in English we often say, 'he is working better now', thinking of a time past when he worked less well. It is for this reason that the sentence, 'He is becoming strong every day', is clearly wrong, when 'every day' is added, 'stronger' must be used.

12. ✗ There is a **best** teacher in that class.

    ✓ There is a **very good** teacher in that class.

    C — Best is used when we compare one with many; not in a non-comparative statement.

13. ✗ He will spend **his future life** here.

    ✓ He will spend **his remaining life** here.

    ✓ He will spend **the rest of his life** here.

    C — For the *rest of his life* we may use *his remaining life*. As an adjective *future* means 'at a later time.'

14.
- ✗ This is a **worth-seeing sight**.
- ✓ This is a **sight worth-seeing**.
- C When we use *worth* to suggest that a specified course of action is advisable, we use it after *worth*, and not before it.

15.
- ✗ We have never seen **a so good boy**.
- ✓ We have never seen **so good a boy**.
- C When so is used in the sense of '*to such a great extent*', it modifies the whole noun phrase and comes before it.

16.
- ✗ He got nearly **cent per cent** marks.
- ✓ He got nearly **full** marks.
- C *Cent per cent* is non-gradable and cannot be modified by *nearly* or *almost, full*, means containing as much or as many as possible.

17.
- ✗ He **is** best player.
- ✓ He **is the** best player.
- C A superlative adjective (e.g. *best*) is always preceded by *the*.

18.
- ✗ The New Delhi **is** big city.
- ✓ New Delhi **is a big** city.

	C	Names of most cities are not preceded by a definite article in English.
19.	✗	I live **in the** Delhi.
	✓	I live **in** Delhi.
	C	**We not use definite article 'the' with proper nouns**. Delhi is the name of a place, therefore it is a proper noun.
20.	✗	**The man** is a member of the society.
	✓	**Man** is a member of society.
	C	*Man* and *society* are used in a generic sense and do not need an article.
21.	✗	We should love **the god**.
	✓	We should love **God**.
	C	When the term 'God' refers to the supreme being who is believed to have created this universe, **we do not use 'the' before it**.
22.	✗	She got **an employment** there.
	✓	She got **employment** there.
	C	As an abstract noun, *employment* does not need an indefinite article.
23.	✗	We should not make **noise**.
	✓	We should not make a **noise**.

✓ *Noise* can be used as a mass noun as well as a countable noun. As a countable noun it means 'a loud or unpleasant sound' and is preceded by a.

24. ✗ I have **an urgent** business.

    ✓ I have **urgent** business or **some urgent** business.

    C Business is not a countable noun and cannot be preceded by an indefinite article.

25. ✗ What **a fun**!

    ✓ What **fun**!

    C As a mass noun, *fun* does need an indefinite article.

26. ✗ We had **picnic**.

    ✓ We had **a picnic**.

    C As a countable noun, *picnic* needs an article before it.

27. ✗ Every **people** know this.

    ✓ Every **man** or **person** knows this.

    ✓ **Everyone** knows this.

    C *People* is a collective noun and refers to human beings in general. It cannot be quantified by every.

28. ✗ He held the book in **the both** hands.

   ✓ He held the book in **both** hands/**both his** hands.

   C Both is all inclusive and therefore definite. It does not need a definite article.

29. ✗ An idle man should do **some or other work**.

   ✓ An idle man should do **some work or another**.

   C *Some work or another* is a fixed expression and can not be changed.

30. ✗ Shakespeare is greater than any other **poets**.

   ✓ Shakespeare is greater than any other **poet**.

   C *Any*, when used with a countable noun, means 'a single' and cannot co-occur with a plural noun in a noun phrase.

31. ✗ He is in class **ninth**.

   ✓ He is in class **nine**/the **ninth class**.

   C When used to qualify a noun, an ordinal number (e.g. *ninth*) precedes it and a cardinal number (e.g. *nine*) follows it.

32. ✗ This article costs **rupees ten**.

    ✓ This article costs **ten rupees**.

    C Though a cardinal number, *ten* cannot follow rupee because we are talking about the whole amount, and not the last rupee (i.e. the ***tenth rupee***).

33. ✗ He came a 2nd time.

    ✓ He came a second time.

    C The rules given below will help in understanding when to write numbers in words and when in figures:

    (a) Write the numbers of kings and queens in R characters thus - Henry II.

    (b) **Write ordinal numbers to 'twelfth' in words, except in dates.**

    (c) Write dates thus, July 7 or 7th July, and not the 7th of July or the seventh of July.

    (d) Write cardinal numbers up to twelve in words, except when telling the time, e.g. 11 p.m.

    (e) **Write cardinal and ordinal numbers above twelve and twelfth in either words or figures as seems in each case the more convenient.**

34.
- ✗ King George **the sixth**.
- ✓ King George **VI**.
- C See (a) in 33.

35.
- ✗ Raipur is **hot** than Simla.
- ✓ Raipur is hotter than Simla.
- C In comparison, use the comparative degree of the adjective in use.

36.
- ✗ Horse is **usefuller** than car.
- ✓ A horse is **more useful** than a car.
- C When an adjective is a compound word (e.g. *useful*), we use *more* in the comparative and *most* in the superlative degree.

37.
- ✗ From the two he is clever.
- ✓ He is the **more** clever **of the two**.
- ✓ He is the **cleverer of the two**.
- C When we compare two persons the adjective cannot be in the positive form, it must be comparative.

38.
- ✗ **From the three** he is more clever.
- ✓ He is the **cleverest of** the three.
- C When more than two persons are compared, the relevant adjective is in the superlative form.

39.
- ✗ He had **leave of** four days.
- ✓ He had four days' **leave**.
- ✓ He had **leave for** four days.
- C *Four days' leave restricts* the nature of leave, and must be either in the genitive form or a prepositional complement.

40.
- ✗ I **am hopeless** to pass.
- ✓ I **have no hope** of passing.
- C *I am hopeless* means *I feel despair* which is a complete sentence and does not need a complement.

41.
- ✗ He was a so **big man** that he could not sit in this chair.
- ✓ He was so **big a man** that he could not sit in this chair.
- C The sentense requries the article.

42.
- ✗ **Yours affectionate** friend.
- ✓ **Your affectionate** friend.
- ✓ **Yours affectionately**.
- C If *affectionate* qualifies *friend*, to form a noun phrase, we will use *your* (and not yours). If *affectionately* is used, *yours* (rather *than your*) is used. *Yours affectionately* is a formal ending of a letter.

43.
- ✗ The country is **plain**.
- ✓ The country is **flat** (**or level**).
- C *Plain* means 'simple' or 'base' where as *flat* means 'having a level surface'

44.
- ✗ Your **lovely** friend.
- ✓ Your **loving** friend.
- C 'Lovely' means attractive and 'loving' means affectionate; in this context, **lovely** is absolutely inappropriate. However, if the reference is to a friend who is lovely one can say, 'I met your lovely friend'.

45.
- ✗ We live in **tribal** area.
- ✓ We live in a (**or the**) **tribal** area.
- C Given below are examples of the innumerable mistakes made by misuse of 'the' and 'a'. Any good English grammar gives the rules for the use and omission of the articles: My attempt to make these rules as simple for Indian students as possible runs as follows:

  (a) Is the noun used a proper or a common noun?

  (b) Remember that a noun can be proper in one sentence and common in another; so it is useless to label a particular noun as proper or common.

(c) If the noun used is proper it will take no article.

(d) If it is common it must have an article, except in the use of (e) below.

(e) If the common noun is not the name of one particular person or thing, it requires the indefinite article 'a' when the noun is singular; when plural, 'a' is never used and usually no article is required, though 'some' sometimes takes its place.

(f) There are several phrases, most of them prepositional (e.g., 'in view of', 'on condition that') or verbal (e.g., 'to put heart into', 'to keep house for'), in which nouns, usually common, must be used without articles. The reason is that these are frozen expressions which do not permit any internal change. For all practical purposes they may be treated as one word of special meaning,

46. ✗ I mean London in **USA**.

✓ I mean the London in the **USA**.

C ***London***, a proper name will not need

an article. However, if we have to specify one place out of many bearing the same name, it is preceded by the.

47. ✗ I live in **the Bengal**.
    ✓ I live in **Bengal**.
    C *Bengal* a proper name, needs no article.

48. ✗ **The gold** is yellow.
    ✓ **Gold** is yellow.
    C Names of metal do not need an article.

49. ✗ **Himalayas** are mountains.
    ✓ **The Himalayas** are mountains.
    C *The Himalayas* represent a range of mountains, and not a single mountain.

50. ✗ **The mankind** should love the nature.
    ✓ **Mankind** should love nature.
    C Generic expressions such as **man** or **mankind** don't need articles.

51. ✗ Many are **Gods** of Hinduism.
    ✓ Many are **the gods** of Hinduism.

	C	***God*** (with a capital G) is a unique concept in Christianity and other monotheistic religions whereas ***god*** (with small ***g***) is a deity.
52.	✗	He found **hundred** rupees.
	✓	He found a **hundred** rupees.
	C	***One hundred*** is expressed as a ***hundred*** (and not just hundred).
53.	✗	**Ganges** is a river.
	✓	**The Ganges** is a river.
	C	Since Ganges is a river in the Himalayas out of several streams, in English it is called 'the Ganges', in Hindi it is called Ganga.
54.	✗	We had **a picnics** nearly every day.
	✓	We had **picnics** nearly every day.
	C	***Picnics***, a plural noun, cannot be preceded by ***a***.
55.	✗	He won a **running** cup.
	✓	He won a **challenge** cup.
	C	This is a common misuse of the word 'running'. A running cup means a cup given for running. **A cup held only until the date of the next tournament is a *challenge cup*.**

56. ✗ Each of us loves **our or their** home.

    ✓ Each of us loves **his** home.

    C **'Each' is singular in number**. The phrase 'each of us' refers to every single member of a big group or section. **Therefore, 'each of us' will have a singular verb and pronoun**.

57. ✗ None of the boys had learnt **their** lesson.

    ✓ None of the boys had learnt **his** lesson.

    C Since, *none* means *not any one*, it refers to a single entity and needs a singular possession referring to it.

58. ✗ People often spend **his** leisure in cinemas.

    ✓ People often spend **their** leisure in cinemas.

    C **'The word people is collective noun and will always take plural pronouns** such as, 'they', 'their', 'them', etc.

59. ✗ Much efforts **bring their** reward.

    ✓ Much effort **brings its** reward.

    C *Much* indicates quantity and cannot be used with a plural noun. *Efforts* can be used as a countable as well as mass noun (e.g., many efforts were made).

60. ✗ Many villagers cannot write **his** own name.

✓ Many villagers cannot write **their** own name.

C 'Many' is a plural word and can occur with a countable noun (e.g villages). The plural, noun phrase will take pronouns such as 'their', 'them', 'these' etc.

61. ✗ **Each and every** person wore a hat.

✓ **Each** person wore a hat.

✓ **Everybody** wore a hat.

C **'Each and every' can be used together correctly only to convey very strong emphasis.** Indian students are too fond of using both together even when only one of the two adjectives is required.

62. ✗ We want a **sifting** inquiry.

✓ We want a **thorough** inquiry.

C *Sift* as a verb means to examine thoroughly. *Sifting* is a noun it is not used as an adjective. 'Exhaustive' is an alternative to 'thorough'.

63.
- ✗ The horse is **laming**.
- ✓ The horse is **lame**.
- C 'Limping' is **correct** but there is no English adjective '*Laming*'.

WITH VERBS

1.
- ✗ He asked **that what are** you doing.
- ✓ He asked **what we were** doing.
- C **In the reported (or indirect) speech the verb changes to the past tense**. If the verb of the main clause is in the past tense and if the embedded clause begins with a *wh* word, *that* is obligatorily deleted. The verb 'are' which is the present tense changes to 'were' denoting past tense.

2.
- ✗ She asked **had we** taken our food.
- ✓ She asked **if we** had taken our food.
- ✓ She asked **whether we** had taken our food.
- C In the reported speech the word order of an interrogative sentence is changed into that of an assertive sentence. If it was a *yes* or *no* question the embedded clause would begin with *if* or *whether*.

3.
- ✗ Rita said **can** she **go** home.
- ✓ Rita asked if she **could go** home.
- **C** As the main verb is in the past tense, the reported speech has to have the verb in the past tense. The word *order* is changed because it is a *yes/no* question and the clause begins with if or whether.

4.
- ✗ He **does not care, for** my words.
- ✓ He **pays no attention to** what I say.
- **C** *To care for* means 'to look after' or 'to provide for the needs of someone' whereas to *pay attention* to means 'to notice someone or something' in the given context, *care for* is inappropriate.

5.
- ✗ Jack does **not care for** money.
- ✓ Jack does **not take care of** his money.
- **C** The word 'care' is different and general.

6.
- ✗ He said that he **saw** him last year.
- ✓ He said that he **had seen** him the previous year.
- **C** These are examples of the common failure to use the past perfect tense

form in the reported speech if the main verb of the main clause is in the past tense.

7. ✗ He got angry before I **said** a word.
   ✓ He got angry before I **had said** a word.
   C If an event occurred or was to occur before another event in the past and was mentioned earlier, the other event will be mentioned in the past perfect.

8. ✗ This was going on **since** a long time.
   ✓ This was going on **for** a long time.
   C *If* a period of time is mentioned without a starting point, it is indicated by *for* (*and not since*).

9. ✗ I had been for **walking** yesterday.
   ✓ I went for **a walk** yesterday.
   C We *go for a walk* rather than *for walking*. Secondly, the main verb should be in the past tense and not in past perfect.

10. ✗ If I **did** this **I shall be** wrong.
    ✗ If I **shall do** this I **shall be** wrong.
    ✓ If I **do** this I **shall be** wrong.

> **C** In the conditional sentences, if the verb of the conditional clause is in the past, the verb of the consequent clause should have the past tense form. If the consequent clause is in the future tense, the conditional clause must be in the present tense.

11. ✗ When **I shall go to** Baghdad, I shall see him.

    ✓ When I **go to** Baghdad, I shall see him.

    > **C** For the reasons given above, the conditional clause must be in the present tense.

12. ✗ I have **left** smoking.

    ✓ I have **given up** smoking.

    > **C** *To give up* means to stop doing or consuming something whereas *to leave* means 'to go away from'.

13. ✗ I **left** playing.

    ✓ I **stopped** playing.

    > **C** We can *stop* (i.e. cause something to come to an end) playing but we cannot go away from it.

14. ✗ I **take** my food.

    ✓ I **have** my food.

| | C | We can use *have* in the sense of to have but not *take*, which basically means to gain possession of. |

15.
	✗	He went to school to **know** English.
	✓	He went to school to **learn** English.
	C	*To learn* means 'to **gain** knowledge of' whereas to know means 'to have knowledge of'.

16.
	✗	She knows **to swim**.
	✓	She knows **how to swim**.
	C	She has the knowledge of how to swim rather than of the concept of swimming.

17.
	✗	We should not **cut** jokes in class.
	✓	We should not **make** jokes in class.
	C	*To make joke* is an idiomatic expression *to cut jokes* is not.

18.
	✗	I **said to** him to go.
	✓	I **told** him to go.
	C	To *say* is 'to utter something' whereas to *tell* is to communicate something to someone'.

19.
| | ✗ | He said to go. |
| | ✓ | He told me to go. |

> **C** If he uttered 'to go', he spoke that to someone. Hence, ***tell*** is the correct word.

20.
> **✗** I **told** the teacher to excuse me.
>
> **✓** I **asked** the teacher to excuse me.
>
> **C** We ***ask*** a question and not a request.

21.
> **✗** I **wanted that** he should get leave.
>
> **✗** I want that I should get leave.
>
> **✓** I **wanted** him to get leave.
>
> **✓** I want to get leave.
>
> **C** The correct form depends on who is to get leave. If it is him, ***I wanted him to get leave*** if it is me, ***I wanted*** to get leave.

22.
> **✗** I like to play cricket.
>
> **✓** I **want** to play cricket.
>
> **C** 'Like' in this sentence should be used only to mean 'am fond of' and not to mean wish'.

23.
> **✗** My tooth is **paining**.
>
> **✓** My tooth is **aching**.
>
> **C** ***Pain*** is a general form for disturbing sensation, physical or mental, whereas ***ache*** is a severe, lingering pain.

24.
- ✗ I **have got** a hurt on my leg.
- ✓ I **have hurt** my leg.
- C *Have* can be used as a noun for mental pain. It is a mass noun. However, to get *hurt* is permissible.

25.
- ✗ Rita **gave** a speech.
- ✓ Rita **made** a speech.
- C One *makes* a speech but gives a verdict.

26.
- ✗ John has **given** his examination.
- ✓ John has **taken** his examination.
- C The teacher or the examiner 'gives' the test and **the student 'takes' the test**.

27.
- ✗ The teacher **made** a lecture.
- ✓ The teacher **gave** a lecture.
- C *To give a lecture* means 'to put forward information, or argument, in a lecture. We can make mistakes but not lectures.

28.
- ✗ Rita can now **sit** on a bicycle.
- ✓ Rita can now **ride** a bicycle.
- C Ride means to sit on and contract the movement of something (e.g. a horse, a bike)

29.
- ✗ He got **down** from his bicycle.
- ✓ He got **off** his bicycle.
- C *To get* down means 'to descent'. We can say 'he got down the ladder. *To get off* is 'to dismount' which is the more appropriate expression here.

30.
- ✗ He took **out** his shoes.
- ✓ He took **off** his shoes.
- C *'To take off* means to remove from one's body' whereas *to take out* means, to take something away.

31.
- ✗ Please **see** my book.
- ✓ Please **look** at my book.
- C *To look at* means to direct one's gaze in a specific direction' whereas *to see* means 'to perceive with the eyes'. The former is a conscious effort.

32.
- ✗ She would not **hear** me.
- ✓ She would not **listen** to me.
- C Note the difference between 'hear' & 'listen'. One may hear yet not listen.

33.
- ✗ **Keep** this on the table.
- ✓ **Put** this on the table.
- C *To put* means to place something in a position whereas to *keep* means

Little Red Book of Common Errors 119

to cause to continue in a particular position.

34. ✗ My mother always **put** my money in this box.

 ✓ My mother always **keeps** my money in this box.

 C As mentioned in (33).

35. ✗ He **struck a blow on** his face.

 ✓ He **struck** him in the face.

 ✓ He **hit** him in the face.

 C Since to *strike* means to inflict a blow, with one's hand or weapon and so does one *hit*. Hence 'a blow' is redundant.

36. ✗ I went **for** swimming and **enjoyed**.

 ✓ I went **out** swimming and **enjoyed myself**.

 C *To go out* means to leave a building and go into the open air (for a ride, swimming, etc.)

37. ✗ She **lived** there for a day.

 ✓ She **stayed** there for a day.

 C To *stay* means 'to remain in a place' whereas *to live* means 'to make one's home in a particular place'.

38.
- ✗ He **made** a goal.
- ✓ He **scored** a goal.
- C To *score* means 'to gain a point (e.g. a goal) in a competition, *To make* is inappropriate in such a context.

39.
- ✗ We ought to **make** exercise.
- ✓ We ought to **take** exercise.
- C An *exercise* is an activity carried out (i.e. taken) for a specific purpose; it cannot be made.

40.
- ✗ I hope he **must** come.
- ✓ I hope he **will** come.
- ✓ I am sure he will come.
- C *Must* is used to show mistake and cannot occur with hope. **This error is caused by two alternative idioms being combined**.

41.
- ✗ Iron **finds** in many countries.
- ✓ Iron **is found** in many countries.
- C *Iron* is the object to the verb *find* and the verb must be in passive voice if it is used as a subject.

42.
- ✗ Always **fair out** a written exercise.
- ✓ Always **make a fair copy of a written** exercise.

	C	***Fair out*** is not a verb. We make or prepare a rough or fair copy of something written.
43.	✗	I filled **water in the bucket**.
	✓	I filled **the bucket with water**.
	C	***Fill*** is used to cause a container to become full (with water or something else)
44.	✗	He thought **how is it** made.
	✓	He wondered **how it** was made.
	C	If one desires to know something, the appropriate verb is ***wonder***, and not think. If the reporting is in the past tense, the verb of the reported speech will also be in the past tense.
45.	✗	I must revenge **my enemy**.
	✓	I must take revenge **on my enemy**.
	C	***Revenge*** is rarely used as a verb, the proper expression is to ***take*** (or ***inflict***) revenge on.
46.	✗	Harry **choosed** a book.
	✓	Harry **chose** a book.
	C	The past tense of ***choose*** is ***chose***; it is an irregular verb.

47. ✗ The teacher **marked** what he was doing.

    ✓ The teacher **noticed** what he was doing.

    C To *mark* means to make a visible impression on; to *notice* means to take note of.

48. ✗ He asked to Rama why **your** father is angry.

    ✓ He asked Rama why **his** father was angry.

    C If a clause is in the reported speech, we have to use a third person possession for a second person possessive. Besides we *ask* (not *ask to*) someone.

49. ✗ I do not care **for you** (spoken angrily).

    ✓ I do not care **what you do**.

    C '**I do not care for you**', properly used, **means 'I do not like you as a friend'**. 'I do not care for hockey' means 'I do not enjoy playing hockey'.

50. ✗ He **does not** care for his work.

    ✓ He **takes no** care of his work.

    C *To care for* means 'to look after' or 'provide' which is not meant here.

51. ✗ No one **cared** for him after his wife died.

    ✓ No one **took care** of him after his wife had died.

    C The **misuse of 'care for' is very common** and the above mentioned sentences need much practice.

52. ✗ When I went there I found that the lion **was** disappeared.

    ✓ When I went there I found that the lion **had** disappeared.

    C The *second* clause needs past perfect tense, and not the passive voice.

53. ✗ I did not stop because he **went out** before I arrived.

    ✓ I did not stop because he **had gone** out before I arrived.

    C If the past action occurred prior to another past action and is mentioned, it must be in the past perfect tense.

54. ✗ I met a man who was my tutor **20** years ago.

    ✓ I met a man who was my tutor **twenty** years ago.

    C Cardinal numbers from 1-10 are written in numerical forms, whereas, **ordinal numbers are written in words**.

55. ✗ If I **would have** done this, I **would** have done wrong.

    ✓ If I **had** done this, I **should** have done wrong.

    C The conditional clause cannot be in the future (or the past form of the future) tense.

56. ✗ **Leave** the horse's reins.

    ✓ **Let go** the horse's reins.

    C *Leave* means 'go away from' and *let go* means allow someone to escape or go free.

57. ✗ He had to **leave** his rights.

    ✓ He had to **abandon** (or relinquish) his rights.

    C *To leave* means 'to go away from'. One cannot go away from one's rights but one can *abandon* (i.e. give up) one's rights. **'To leave' is a verb often misused**. Correct uses are: (a) to leave a place, (b) to leave something at some place, (c) to leave someone to do something.

58. ✗ I **take** my food.

    ✓ I **have** my food.

	C	'Take my food' is not wrong, but an **Englishman rarely uses this expression**.
59.	✗	I take your **leave**.
	✓	I must say **goodbye**.
	C	'**I take your leave**' is not wrong, but **is suitable only for a formal occasion**.
60.	✗	In the **noon** I took rest.
	✓	I had a rest in the **middle of the day**.
	C	*To have a rest* is more *colloquial* than to *take rest*. *Noon* refers to twelve o'clock in the day, it is a *point* (rather than *period* of time).
61.	✗	I **came to know** as to how he did this.
	✓	I **learnt** how he did this.
	C	The use of *as to* is superfluous. To *learn* (to gain knowledge of) is a conscious process, *to come to know* is accidental.
62.	✗	I **came to know** why he was sad.
	✓	I **found out** why he was sad.

	C	'Came to know' is a difficult phrase to use correctly and is better avoided.
63.	✗	He went to school to **know** arithmetic.
	✓	He went to school to **learn** arithmetic.
	C	We 'learn' before we 'know'. 'Know' is used when learning is finished.
64.	✗	He **knows to** swim.
	✓	He knows **how** to swim.
	C	He knows the technique or art of swimming rather than what the verb indicates.
65.	✗	Later on he **knew** his mistake.
	✓	Later on he **realised** his mistake.
	C	To *realise*, means 'to, become fully aware of, whereas to *know* means 'to have knowledge or information'.
66.	✗	He **cut** his pencil.
	✓	He **sharpened** his pencil.
	C	*Sharpen* means 'to make something sharp' whereas *to cut* means, 'to make an opening' or 'to remove'.
67.	✗	Shall I **cut** this word?

- ✓ Shall I **scratch** out this word?
- C **To cut** means 'to abridge' or 'remove' whereas to **scratch** means 'to strike out'.

68.
- ✗ They **cut** Charles I's head.
- ✓ They **cut off** Charles I's head.
- C ***Cut*** means 'to make an opening' or 'to remove' but ***cut off*** means 'to remove completely by cutting'.

69.
- ✗ I **asked** my servant to bring water.
- ✓ I **told** my servant to bring water.
- C It is advisable to use '**I told him to...**' only **towards a person to whom you have a right to give an order**, and 'I asked him to...' towards a person of whom you can or want to make a request only.

70.
- ✗ He is **troubling** his subjects.
- ✓ He is **oppressing** his subjects.
- ✓ He is **ill-treating** his subjects.
- C To ***trouble*** means 'to cause distress or anxiety'. It is not an appropriate word in this context.

71.
- ✗ He is **troubling** me.
- ✓ He is **giving me trouble**.

✓	He is **treating me badly**.
✓	He is **bullying** me.
C	To use *trouble* as a verb is not wrong but *to give trouble* is more idiomatic. **To bully** is a stranger term, it means 'to use strength to intimidate someone'.

72.
✗	My foot is **paining**.
✓	**I have a pain** in my foot.
✓	My foot is **hurting**.
C	**'To pain' (verb) should be used transitively only**.

73.
✗	All day I was **putting** on a sweater.
✗	He came **putting** on a smart turban.
✓	All day I was **wearing** a sweater.
✓	He was **wearing** a smart turban.
C	'To put on clothes' refers to the act of dressing, e.g. 'he is in his room putting on his shoes'. Once the act of dressing is over, 'to wear' is used to express the act of carrying clothes on the body.

74.
✗	I cannot **put on** with my work.
✓	I cannot **manage** my work.
C	Put on (add to existing service) cannot be used in the sense of *manage*.

Little Red Book of Common Errors 129

75.
- ✗ I have **ordered** for a new racquet.
- ✓ I have **ordered** a new racquet.
- C When used with an object, **order** does not need a preposition.

76.
- ✗ I have disposed **off** my car.
- ✓ I have disposed **of** my car.
- C ***Dispose* of** means 'to get rid of'. There is no phrasal verb ***dispose off***.

77.
- ✗ I put up **with him** (meaning stayed).
- ✓ He **put me up**.
- C **'To put up with' should be used only to mean to tolerate an annoying person or thing.**

78.
- ✗ People **respected** him at the station.
- ✓ People **treated him with respect** at the station.
- ✓ People **showed respect for** him at the station.
- C **'To respect someone' properly means to have a high opinion of someone's character.**

79.
- ✗ I **had a mind** to play.
- ✓ I **intended** to play.
- C ***To have a mind*** is not an acceptable expression.

130 *Little Red Book of Common Errors*

80.
    - ✗ It **goes hard** with him to do this.
    - ✓ He **finds it hard** to do this.
    - C ***To go hard*** is not an acceptable expression.

81.
    - ✗ We cannot **maintain our livelihood**.
    - ✓ We cannot **earn a living**.
    - ✓ We cannot **get a living**.
    - C ***To maintain*** means 'to keep something at the same level'.

82.
    - ✗ I **persuaded** him to stop but he would not.
    - ✓ I **tried to persuade** him to stop.
    - C ***Persuade*** means to induce someone to do something by reasoning. It is used only if the effort is successful.

83.
    - ✗ I **shot the** tiger **but missed**.
    - ✓ I **missed** the tiger.
    - ✓ I **shot at** the tiger **but missed**.
    - C If you say '**I shot the tiger**', you **mean you hit and probably killed it**.

84.
    - ✗ I went **for shooting** and **enjoyed**.
    - ✓ I went out shooting and **enjoyed myself**.

	C	***To enjoy oneself*** means to have, 'a pleasant time'.
85.	✗	Do not **play mischiefs**.
	✓	Do not **get up to mischief**.
	C	***To play*** means 'to take part in something'; ***To get up*** to means to be occupied in.
86.	✗	I **stood second** in my class.
	✓	I **was second** in my class.
	C	'Stand second' is not wrong but perhaps an Englishman would rarely use it.
87.	✗	I **am reading** at the High School.
	✓	I **am at** the High school.
	C	**'To read' should be used to mean 'to peruse or to study books'**.
88.	✗	He **did** no fault.
	✓	He **committed** no fault.
	C	To ***commit*** means 'To carry out'. We commit a mistake, fault or crime. The ***use*** of *do* is inappropriate.
89.	✗	We **make** drill.
	✓	We **do** drill.

	C	***Drill*** refers to military training exercises. We cannot make drill.
90.	✗	The Council **is consisted** of ten members.
	✓	The Council **consists** of ten members.
	C	***Council of*** (to be composed of) cannot be passivized.
91.	✗	Romulus **found** Rome.
	✓	Romulus **founded** Rome.
	C	The past tense of ***found*** (establish) is founded.
92.	✗	'Where is the book?' 'It is **not found**'.
	✓	'Where is the book?' 'It is **lost**.'
	C	The opposite of to ***find*** is to *lose*.
93.	✗	He **prevented** him from harm.
	✓	He **protected** him from harm.
	C	'Prevent' and 'protect' are often confused. **'Prevent' is used to stop someone from beginning to do harm; 'protect' means to save someone from harm**.
94.	✗	My **leg has been operated**.
	✓	I **have had an operation** on my leg.

| | C | 'To operate' (verb) used **in the sense of to perform a surgical must be followed by 'on'. My leg has been operated 'on'.** |

95.
	✗	It is written in this letter that...
	✓	This letter says that.
	C	**'It is written'** is not wrong, but **is usually clumsy English**.

96.
	✗	He **losed** a rupee.
	✓	He **lost** a rupee.
	C	There are verbs that do not take 'ed' for the past tense. **The past tense of lose is 'lost'.**

97.
	✗	When he comes you must **wish** him.
	✓	When he comes you must **greet** (or welcome) him.
	C	As a verb, ***wish*** needs two objects (e.g I wished him a good day).

98.
	✗	This boy always needs **poking**.
	✓	This boy always needs **pushing along**.
	C	***To poke*** means 'to prod' and is not appropriate here.

99.
| | ✗ | I **gave** him a love-set. |
| | ✓ | I **took** a love-set off him. |

	✓	I **beat** him in a love-set.
	C	You can 'beat' or 'defeat' not take a love-set.
100.	✗	You **can avail** of this.
	✗	This **can be availed** of.
	✓	You **can avail** yourself of this.
	C	One ***avails oneself*** of something; that is the idiom.
101.	✗	Rita is **very much** sorry.
	✓	Rita is **very** sorry.
	C	Both ***very*** and ***much*** are intensified of the same type. Hence, much is redundant.
102.	✗	We scarcely see a lion.
	✓	We rarely see a lion.
	C	***Scarcely*** means 'almost not' whereas ***rarely*** means 'not often'.
103.	✗	I did it **anyhow**.
	✓	I managed to do it **somehow**.
	C	'Anyhow' means 'anyway'. It is used to indicate that something happened or will happen in spite of something else.
104.	✗	Harry told the story in **details**.

- ✓ Harry told the story in **detail**.
- C *In detail* refers to 'in regard to *every* feature or aspect.' It is an adverbial expression.

105.
- ✗ Aeroplanes reach Europe **soon**.
- ✓ Aeroplanes reach Europe **quickly**.
- C *Quickly* means 'at a fast speed' taking short time whereas *soon* means in a short time.

106.
- ✗ Yesterday **in the night** Harry came to dinner.
- ✓ Yesterday **evening** Harry came to dinner.
- C *Evening* refers to the period of time at the end of the *day* usually up to bed time.

107.
- ✗ **Before long** there was no one there.
- ✓ **Long ago** there was no one there.
- C 'Ago' means 'counting from now'; 'before long' means 'soon'.

108.
- ✗ **What for** do you go to school?
- ✓ **What do you** go to school for?
- ✓ Why **do you** go to school?
- C *For what* (reasons) means *why*. As the question word moves to the beginning

of a sentence, the preposition may be left behind.

109.
- ✗ This book is **too** interesting.
- ✓ This book is **very** interesting.
- C *Very* is a neutral intensifier whereas *too* suggests something excessive.

110.
- ✗ He behaved **cowardly**.
- ✓ He behaved in a **cowardly** manner.
- C *Cowardly* is an adjective and cannot be used as an adverb.

111.
- ✗ Silas lives **miserly**.
- ✓ Silas lives in a **miserly** way.
- C *Miserly* is an adjective, the adverbial form is '*in a miserly manner*'.

112.
- ✗ He plays **good**.
- ✓ He plays **well**.
- C *Good* is not used as an adverb just as *well* is not used as an adjective.

113.
- ✗ He plays **good than I**.
- ✓ He plays **better than I**.
- C The comparative degree of *well* is *better*.

114.
- ✗ Hardly I have had any rest **since one** week.

	✓	Hardly **have** I had any rest **for a** week.
	C	When a sentence begins with *hardly*, the first auxiliary of the verb follows *it*.
115.	✗	He was **very kind enough** to invite me.
	✓	He was **so kind** as to invite me.
	✓	He was **kind enough** to invite me.
	C	Both *very* and *enough* cannot be used as the modifier of the same adjective.
116.	✗	**Really speaking** it is not hot.
	✓	**As a matter of fact** it is not hot.
	✓	**To speak the truth** it is not hot.
	✓	**In truth** it is not hot
	✓	**In fact** it is not hot.
	C	*Really* means 'in actual fact', and is not appropriate in this sentence.
117.	✗	To tell **in brief**
	✓	**In short, in brief**.
	C	As *in brief* is used to sum up what is being said, *to tell* is superfluous.
118.	✗	If he fails he will be **nowhere**.

- ✓ If he fails he will get **into great trouble**.
- ✓ If he fails he will be **ruined**.
- C *Nowhere* means 'not in any place' and is inappropriate here.

119.
- ✗ **Just I** had gone when he came.
- ✓ **I had just** gone when he came.
- C As an adverb *just* comes immediately before the main verb.

120.
- ✗ Never **I have** seen such a sight.
- ✓ Never **have I** seen such a sight.
- C If *never* occurs in the beginning of a sentence, it is followed by an auxiliary verb.

121.
- ✗ It is a very good film; I liked **it on the whole**.
- ✓ It is a very good film; I liked **the whole of it**.
- C **'On the whole' is used to sum up your opinion of something which is good and bad in parts.** For instance, "The photography of the film was bad but the plot was exciting. On the whole I enjoyed it.'

WITH CONJUNCTIONS

1. ✗ Though he is **fat yet he** runs fast.

   ✓ Though he is **fat**, he runs fast.

   C 'Though' is the conjunction and **a second conjunction —'but', 'yet' or, 'still'—is not required**.

2. ✗ If he is **fat then he** will run slowly.

   ✓ If he is **fat, he** will run slowly.

   C If then is *if*. In a conditional clause the consequent clause need not have ***then***.

3. ✗ As I fired at the **tiger at that time he** shook my arm.

   ✓ As I fired at the **tiger, he** shook my arm.

   C The first clause refers to a point of time, its repetition (at that time) is redundant.

4. ✗ Because he is clever **therefore** (or so) he gets good marks.

   ✓ Because he is clever, he gets good marks.

   C In a ***cause***-effect sentence, if the cause is indicated by ***because***, the result clause does not need ***therefore***.

5. ✗ He did not come to school. **Because**

he was ill.

✓ He did not come to school, because he was ill.

C The clause that indicates the cause, cannot be separated from the clause that indicates its effect.

6. ✗ No sooner **I had spoken** than he left.

✓ No sooner **had I spoken** than he left.

C Just like *never*, if a sentence begins with *no sooner* the auxiliary precedes the subject.

7. ✗ I have bought many fireworks as **rockets and etc**.

✓ I have bought many fireworks **such as rockets**.

C It would be good if that overworked Latin abbreviation 'etc' was forbidden in all composition.

8. ✗ I want to know **as to why** I have been detained.

✓ I want to know **why** I have been detained.

C In modern English *as to* is not needed to connect a clause with the main clause.

9. ✗ This is my friend, he was at school with me.

   ✓ This is my friend **who** was at school with me.

   C *Who* is needed if the relative clause is attached to the noun phrase ***my friend***.

10. ✗ This is my servant, I was telling you about him.

    ✓ This is my servant **about whom** I was telling you.

    C As the second clause is a relative clause, it must be attached by **who** (or that) to the noun phrase *my servant*.

11. ✗ Supposing **if he** fails, what will he do?

    ✓ Supposing **he** fails what will he do?

    ✓ If he fails what will **he do**?

    C As ***supposing*** and ***if*** have the same function, only one of them should be used.

12. ✗ Until he does not try, he must be punished.

    ✓ He must be punished **until** he tries.

    ✓ He must be punished **so long as he does not try**.

	C	*Until*, means up to the point in time or the event mentioned. It is normally used in the beginning of the clause.
13.	✗	Not only **he will go**, but **also he will** remain there.
	✓	Not only **will he go**, but **he will also** remain there.
	C	Like '*never*' and **no sooner not only** attracts the auxiliary verb to its immediate right if it occurs in the beginning of a sentence.
14.	✗	He **neither comes** nor he **writes**.
	✓	**Neither does** he come **nor does** he write.
	C	'He neither comes nor writes' is equally correct and probably more common. But the rule is that **when the first word of the sentence is a negative the auxiliary verb must be inverted, as in a direct question**.
15.	✗	I am fond of all games **as for an example** cricket.
	✓	I am fond of all games, **for example**, cricket.
	C	*As*, is redundant here because we don't need a conjunction.

16.
   - ✗ She called me **as a** fool.
   - ✓ She called me **a** fool.
   - C *As* is redundant here as well.

17.
   - ✗ He is the fastest runner **and he** came last.
   - ✓ He is the fastest runner **but** he came last.
   - C **'But' is the conjunction to be used when the second clause gives information contrary to the one expected by the first clause.....**

18.
   - ✗ He was angry **therefore** I ran away.
   - ✓ He was angry **so** I ran away.
   - C ***Therefore*** refers to a logical conclusion whereas *so* means 'and for this reason'

19.
   - ✗ I was trying to work, **at that time** he was disturbing me.
   - ✓ While I was trying to work, **he** was disturbing me.
   - C ***While*** signals a point (or period) of time something was happening.

20.
   - ✗ This is my house, **I live here**.
   - ✓ This is my house **where I live**.
   - C 'I live here' defines the house and needs to be relationed.

21.
- ✗ This is an interesting book, **I am reading** it.
- ✓ The book **which I am reading** is interesting
- C The relation clause must be attached to the noun it is about.

22.
- ✗ I am glad for tomorrow is holiday.
- ✓ I am glad because tomorrow **is a** holiday.
- C As the second is the reason, it should be attached to the main clause by *because*, *for* can be used as a conjunction in place of *because* or *since* in some cases.

WITH PREPOSITIONS

1.
- ✗ This paper is inferior than that.
- ✓ This paper is inferior to that.
- C With *inferior* and *superior* the comparative mark of preposition is *to*.

2.
- ✗ I *am ill since* three months.
- ✓ I **have been ill** for three months.
- ✓ I **have been ill since** July.
- C When reckoning from a particular date we use 'since', e.g., 'since last

Friday', 'since July 8th' but we always use 'for' for a period, e.g., 'for a week', 'for a long time'.

3. ✗ This is my **first time to play** cricket since a long time.

   ✓ I **have not played** cricket for a long time.

   ✓ This is my **first game** of cricket **for** a long time.

   C For a period of time without a fixed starting point, we use *for*.

4. ✗ This is different **to that**.

   ✓ This is different from **that**.

   C *Different* takes the preposition *from*.

5. ✗ This resembles **to that**.

   ✓ This resembles **that**.

   C No preposition is used between *resembles* and its object.

6. ✗ Everyone should **pray God**.

   ✓ Everyone should **pray to God**.

   C Between *pray* and its object we use *to*.

7. ✗ He wrote **me**.

   ✓ He wrote to **me**.

| C | Between *write* and its indirect object we use to (e.g. He wrote a letter to *me*) |

8.
✗	I shall explain **them this**.
✓	I shall explain **this to them**.
C	Between *explain* and its indirect object, we use to.

9.
✗	Send this letter **on** my address.
✓	Send this letter **to** my address.
C	If a verb needs a direct (e.g. *this letter*) and an indirect object, we use *to* before the indirect object (e.g. *to me*).

10.
✗	He suggested **me this**.
✓	He suggested **this to me**.
C	If a verb has a direct and a indirect object, the latter comes after the direct object and is preceded by *to*.

11.
✗	He goes **in** the school.
✓	He goes **to** school.
C	The destination of movement is indicated by *to*.

12.
| ✗ | He goes **on** his work. |
| ✓ | He goes **to** his work. |
| C | If the order is changed, *to* is not used,

e.g. He gave **me a book**.

13.
- ✗ He **called** me in dinner.
- ✓ He **invited** me to dinner.
- C *Invite* is a polite word for a formal request to come. We always *invite* someone to something.

14.
- ✗ He reached **to Delhi**.
- ✓ He reached **Delhi**.
- C Between the verb *reach* and its destination, no preposition is used.

15.
- ✗ He told **to** me to go.
- ✓ He told me to go.
- C Between *tell* and its objects, no preposition is used.

16.
- ✗ She did not **ask any question to him**.
- ✓ She did not **ask him any question**.
- C *Ask* needs two objects. Usually the indirect object comes first and needs no preposition.

17.
- ✗ Harry will be cured **from** his fever.
- ✓ Harry will be cured **of** his fever.
- C With *cure* we use the preposition *of*.

18.
- ✗ He threw the stick **in** the river.

	✓	He threw the stick **into** the river.
	C	If the object thrown is likely to go inside, we use the preposition *into*.
19.	✗	He rides **in** a cycle.
	✓	He rides **on** a cycle.
	✗	He sat **on** a tree.
	✓	He sat **in** a tree.
	C	**We use 'on' when we mean 'on top of'**, e.g., 'on a horse'. We use 'in' 'when we mean inside something, e.g. 'in an aeroplane'.
20.	✗	There is no harm **to do** this.
	✓	There is no harm **in doing** this.
	C	After *harm* the verb of compliment is in the present particle form which is preceded by *in*.
21.	✗	Write **with** ink.
	✓	Write **in** ink.
	C	We say write *with* a pen *in* ink.
22.	✗	He rides **on** a car.
	✓	He rides **in** a car.
	C	If you use 'on' here, the sense will be 'on top of the car'. **But one can 'ride inside the car' and not 'on top of the car'**. Here 'in' is appropriate.

23.
    - ✗ This is a comfortable house **to live**.
    - ✓ This is a comfortable house **to live in**.
    - C *To live in is* a phrasal verb which means 'to reside'.

24.
    - ✗ This is the road **to go**.
    - ✓ This is the road **to go by**.
    - C We always *go by* a road.

25.
    - ✗ He gave me a gun **to shoot**.
    - ✓ He gave me a gun **to shoot** with.
    - C The full expression is 'to shoot with a gun'.

26.
    - ✗ I gave him a chair **to sit**.
    - ✓ I gave him a chair **to sit on**.
    - C One *sits on* (or *in*) a chair.

27.
    - ✗ He married **with an** American lady.
    - ✓ He married **an** American lady.
    - C If we are *reporting* that he took someone as his wife, we say, *he married her*. *He is married to her* indicates that they are married.

28.
    - ✗ They are called **with** different names.
    - ✓ They are called **by** different names.

	C	*To call by* means to address (someone) *as*.
29.	✗	Harry accompanied **with his** friends.
	✓	Harry accompanied **his** friends.
	C	In the active voice, *accompany* needs no preposition before its object.
30.	✗	We should not spend money **for** luxuries.
	✓	We should not spend money **on** luxuries.
	C	*Spend* needs *on* before the object.
31.	✗	He went away **for** doing some business.
	✓	He went away **on** business.
	C	*On business* means 'in some trade or regular profession'.
32.	✗	He went **for riding**.
	✓	He went for **a ride**.
	✓	He went **riding**.
	C	Either we use *ride* as a noun (in which case we say, '*for a ride*') or we use the gerund form of the verb (e.g. riding).
33.	✗	We discussed **on the** matter.
	✓	We discussed **the** matter.

	C	***Discuss*** needs no preposition before its object.
34.	✗	He is angry **on** me.
	✗	He is pleased **on me**.
	✓	He is angry **with** me.
	✓	He is pleased **with me**.
	C	With ***to be angry or pleased*** we use ***with***.
35.	✗	He asked **a** holiday.
	✓	He asked **for a** holiday.
	C	We always ask someone for ***something***.
36.	✗	I shall inform them **this**.
	✓	I shall inform them **of this**.
	C	We ***inform someone of something***.
37.	✗	Our college is built **by** bricks.
	✓	Our college is built **of** bricks.
	C	***To build*** means to construct something by putting some materials. A building is made of those materials.
38.	✗	**Due** to illness, I cannot go to school.
	✓	**Owing** to illness, I cannot go to school.

	C	Owing to means 'on account of' whereas ***due to*** means 'caused by'.
39.	✗	He was prevented **to** come.
	✓	He was prevented **from** coming.
	C	We are always prevented (stopped) from doing something.
40.	✗	He walked five miles **by** foot.
	✓	He walked five miles **on** foot.
	C	We always ***walk on foot*** when we do not use any transport.
41.	✗	I **met with** your friend there.
	✓	I **met** your friend there.
	C	***To meet*** means 'to happen to come in the company of someone', ***to meet*** with means to have a meeting with'.
42.	✗	My brother is superior **than** you in strength.
	✓	My brother is superior **to** you in strength.
	C	***Superior*** and ***inferior*** take ***to*** and not ***than*** as a comparative mark.
43.	✗	Diwali corresponds **with** Christmas.
	✓	Diwali corresponds **to** Christmas.
	C	***To corresponds*** means 'to have a close similarity' whereas t***o correspond with*** means ***to communicate***'.

44.	✗	I am obliged of you **by** this good turn.
	✓	I am obliged to you **for** this good turn.
	C	***Oblige*** always takes ***to*** before its object.
45.	✗	He went **near** the station.
	✓	He went **to** the station.
	C	If his destination was the station, he went ***to*** the station ***near*** indicates proximity.
46.	✗	He **was** favourite with his friends.
	✓	He **was a** favourite with his friends.
	C	As a countable noun, ***favourite*** to used from preferred to all others of the same kind, and needs an article.
47	✗	**From** our class he did best.
	✓	He did best **in** our class.
	C	When used with a verb (like ***do***), ***best*** means 'the most successful result'.
48.	✗	The term begins **from** July 1st.
	✓	The term begins **on** July 1st.
	C	***Term begin*** refers to a point of starting at a certain time.
49.	✗	He will be cured **from** his fever.
	✓	He will be cured **of** his fever.

| C | As a verb *cure* is followed by *of* to link it to its object. |

50.
✗	There are many advantages **from** this.
✓	The advantages **of** this are many.
C	*Advantage* (i.e. the opportunity to gain something) needs *of*.

51.
✗	There is a saying **in** the Hindus.
✓	There is a saying **among** the Hindus.
C	*Among* means 'occurring in' or 'shared' by.

52.
✗	We waste much time **in** trifles.
✓	We waste much time **on** (or over) trifles.
C	We waste time *on* something, not inside it.

53.
✗	I pitied **on him**.
✓	I pitied **him**.
C	The verb *pity* does not use a preposition before its object.

54.
✗	He angried **on** me.
✓	He was angry **with** me.
C	*Angry* can not be used as a verb. As an adjective, it is accompanied by *with*.

Little Red Book of Common Errors 155

55. ✗ When this was **searched** it was found.

    ✓ When this was **searched** for, it was found.

    C We always *search* for something. *Search* in the sense of examine needs no *for*.

56. ✗ I **searched** the man.

    ✓ I **searched for** the man.

    C This is correct only when it means 'I looked in his pockets' or something similar.

57. ✗ He went to the **back side** of the house.

    ✓ He went **behind** the house.

    ✓ He went to the **back** of the house.

    C *Back, front, behind* indicate side and the use of side is redundant here.

58. ✗ The Post Office will compensate the **loss**.

    ✓ The Post Office will compensate us **for the loss**.

    C We always *compensate* someone for something.

59. ✗ I must go; there is no **help**.

	✓	I must go; there is no **help for it**.
	C	*Help* here refers to the fact of being useful (for something).
60.	✗	There was a match between Bombay **against** Madras.
	✓	There was a match between Bombay **and** Madras.
	C	**This common mistake seems to be caused by mixing up of two expressions**. You could say, 'There was a match, Bombay against Madras'.
61.	✗	There was a fight **with** Ram and Hari yesterday.
	✓	There was a fight **between** Ram and Hari yesterday.
	C	*Between* suggest a relationship involving two or more parties.
62.	✗	The First World War was fought **during** 1914-18.
	✓	The First World War was fought **between** 1914 and 1918.
	C	*During* refers to a duration of time. If two points of time is to be emphasized *between* is preferred.
63.	✗	England grew prosperous **between** Queen Victoria's reign.

✓ England grew prosperous **during** Queen Victoria's reign.

C Practise using 'during' and 'between' correctly. **Two 'points of time' must be mentioned if you want to use 'between'.**

SOME MISLEADING PARTS OF SPEECH

Problem-Causing Pronouns

1. ✗ Invite **she** for the picnic.
   ✓ Invite **her** for the picnic.
   C If a personal pronoun (e.g *she*) is the object to a verb, it is used in its objective form (e.g. *her*.)

2. ✗ He and **me** are going to the movie today.
   ✗ Her and **me** were eating.
   ✓ He and **I** are going to the movie today.
   ✓ She and **I** were eating.
   C 'I' is one of the subjective form and should not be put in the objective form (e.g. *me*), if it is the subject.

3. ✗ **Them** and I participated in the competition together.
   ✓ **They** and I participated in the competition together.
   C The subjective form of *them* is *they*.

4. ✗ This should be kept between you and **she**.

- ✓ This should be kept between you and **her**.
- C The objective form of ***she*** is ***her***; it is object to the preposition ***between***.

5.
- ✗ **I and my wife** were declared the best couple dancer.
- ✓ **My wife and I** were declared the best couple dancer.
- C If 'I' is one of the conjoined subjects, it comes at the last element of the conjoined noun phrase.

6.
- ✗ **Us** students have boycotted the examinations.
- ✓ **We** students have boycotted the examinations.
- C ***We*** is the subject of the sentence and cannot be in the objective form.

7.
- ✗ Why do you always have to come between **she and I**?
- ✓ Why do you always have to come between **her and me**?
- C The object to the preposition ***between*** is to be in objective form, i.e. ***me***.

8.
- ✗ We thought that **you and her** would come to receive us at the airport.
- ✓ We thought that **you and she** would come to receive us at the airport.
- C The expression ***you and she*** is the subject of the embedded clause.

9.	✗	What did they present **you and she**?
	✓	What did they present **you and her**?
	C	***Her*** is the object to the verb ***present***, and will be in the objective form.
10.	✗	His girls look just like *he*.
	✓	His girls look just like **him**.
	C	***Him*** is the object to the phrasal verb ***look like***.
11.	✗	Let him and **we** show them what we are.
	✓	***Let*** him and **us** show them what we are.
	C	Let means 'allows' and the noun phrase that follows it ***him and me*** is its object.
12.	✗	**I and he** are living together.
	✓	He **and I** are living together.
	C	Courtesy demands that the speaker puts himself as the last contingent of the subject noun phrase (e.g. ***he*** and ***I***).
13.	✗	You are as mean as **me**.
	✓	You are as mean as **I**.
	C	The full expression is 'you are as mean as I ***am***'.

14.
   - ✗ It was **her** who was standing there!
   - ✓ It was **she** who was standing there!
   - C *She* is referred to by *who* which is the subject of the embedded sentence. The sentence is basically of the form 'she was standing there'.

15.
   - ✗ I was very sure that **his** would come to meet me.
   - ✓ I was very sure that **he** would come to meet me.
   - C As *he* is the subject of the embedded clause, it cannot be in the possessive form.

16.
   - ✗ His lecture was better than **me**.
   - ✓ His lecture was better than **mine**.
   - C *Mine* stands for *my* lecture which is in the predicative possession form.

17.
   - ✗ It was **me** who dumped him.
   - ✓ It was **I** who dumped him.
   - C *I* stands for *who*, the subject of the sentence.

18.
   - ✗ None of them **have** listened to what was said.
   - ✓ None of them **has** listened to what was said.

	C	None (not anyone) is singular and needs a singular verb.
19.	✗	There is a lot of dissimilarity between **you and he**.
	✓	There is a lot of dissimilarity between **you and him**.
	C	Both *you* and *him* are object to the preposition *between*.
20.	✗	You should call **our** brother to the party
	✓	You should call **your** brother to the party.
	C	The reference is to the other.
21.	✗	Each must contribute what **they** can.
	✓	Each must contribute what **he** can.
	C	*Each* refers to a singular entity and the appropriate personal pronoun is *he* or *she*.
22.	✗	**I, you and he** should start something together.
	✓	**You, he and I** should start something together.
	C	As a matter of courtesy, **I** should be the last element of the subject noun phrase.

23.	✗	**You, he and me** will remain like this forever.
	✓	**You, he and I** will remain like this forever.
	C	Since, *me* is a part of the noun phrase which is the subject of the sentence, it should be *I*.
24.	✗	**Whom**, according to you has stolen the gold?
	✓	**Who**, according to you has stolen the gold?
	C	*Whom* is the object form of *who*; it cannot be used in the subject positive.
25.	✗	**Whom** do you think will top this year?
	✓	**Who** do you think will top this year?
	C	*Who* is the subject of the predicate *will top this year* and should be formally a subject (*who*, not *whom*).
26.	✗	Did you see **whom** he was?
	✓	Did you see **who** he was?
	C	Since it is the subject of the embedded clause it should be *who*.
27.	✗	Were you expecting **her and I** at the party?

	✓	Were you expecting **her and me** at the party?
	C	As an object to the verb *expect*, I *becomes me*
28.	✗	I looked at **she** and she at **I**.
	✓	I looked at **her and she** at **me**.
	C	In the embedded clause *I* is the object of *look at* and should have the objective form *me*.
29.	✗	Everyone donated something, except **he**.
	✓	Everyone donated something, except **him**.
	C	He is the subject of the deleted embedded clause, but is the object to the preposition *except*, hence, *him*.
30.	✗	He is careless about **her** belongings.
	✓	He is careless about **his** belongings.
	C	*Her* is wrong only if *he* is talking about *his* belongings, and not of his wife's.
31.	✗	**Who** were you looking at?
	✓	**Whom** were you looking at?
	C	*Whom* is the object to the verb *look at*, However, in such constructions *who* is also used.

32.
- ✗ Who did you see in the hall?
- ✗ Who did you give my things to?
- ✓ Whom did you see in the hall?
- ✓ Whom did you give my things to?
- C Formally **whom** is the objective form of **who**. As in both the sentences, **who** is the object to the verb see, it should be **whom** but in modern English, we use who if the objective form occurs in the beginning of a sentence.

33.
- ✗ Don't you know **whom** was awarded last year on the same night?
- ✓ Don't you know **who** was awarded last year on the same night?
- C **Who** occurs in the subject position in the embedded clause and cannot be replaced by **whom**.

34.
- ✗ **Who** would you select as your leader?
- ✓ **Whom** would you select as your leader?
- C Though **whom** is formally correct, **who** is used more frequently these days.

35.
- ✗ **Whom** do you think will be the most suitable for the position?
- ✓ **Who** do you think will be the most suitable for the position?

Little Red Book of Common Errors

	C	***Who*** is the subject of the embedded clause (... will be ...) and cannot be replaced by whom.
36.	✗	**Whom** do you think was the best actor in the play?
	✓	**Who** do you think was the best actor in the play?
	C	***Who*** is the subject of the embedded clause.
37.	✗	**Who** do you want to see now?
	✓	**Whom** do you want to see now?
	C	Though ***whom*** (the objective form) is formally correct, ***who*** is frequently used.
38.	✗	**Who** do you wish to talk with?
	✓	**Whom** do you wish to talk with?
	C	As in (37).
39.	✗	Let me know **whom** do you like the best.
	✓	Let me know **who** do you like the best.
	C	Though ***whom*** is the object of ***like***, ***who*** is frequently used form now.
40.	✗	**Whom** do you think is a real life heroine?

	✓	**Who** do you think is a real life heroine?
	C	**Who** is the subject of the embedded clause and cannot be replaced by **whom**.
41.	✗	We all hated **each other**.
	✓	We all hated **one another**.
	C	**We all** suggest more than two, **one another** is the only appropriate option.
42.	✗	Whom do you think has done this to us?
	✓	Who do you think has done this to us?
	C	**Who** is the subject of the embedded clause.
43.	✗	If I were him, I would have run away long time back.
	✓	If I were he, I would have run away long time back.
	C	In equation sentences i.e. with verb **to be** both pronouns will have the same form, i.e., subjective **I** and **he**.
44.	✗	Rita was as good a singer as **her**.
	✓	Rita was as good a singer as **she**.

| C | ***She*** is the subject of the deleted predicate ***was*** a good singer. |

45.
✗	You cannot tell ***us*** people what to drink.
✓	You cannot tell **we** people what to drink.
✓	You cannot tell us what to drink.
C	In ***us***, people is redundant.

MISTAKES IN THE USE OF ADJECTIVES

1.
✗	When I called Harry, he said that he was not feeling **finely**.
✓	When I called Harry, he said that he was not feeling **fine**.
C	***Finely*** does not exist as an adverb, ***fine*** is both an adjective and an adverb.

2.
✗	I need a large piece of a **course** cloth.
✓	I need a large piece of a **coarse** cloth.
C	***Course*** means 'direction' and is a noun. ***Coarse*** means 'rough' and is the correct word in this context.

3.
| ✗ | He threw a party on his birthday **as usually**. |
| ✓ | He threw a party on his birthday **as usual**. |

	C	*Usually*, an adverb, means 'habitually'; **Usual** is an adjective. We can say *as usual* but not as *usually*.
4.	✗	I dislike **cleverly** children.
	✓	I dislike **clever** children.
	C	*Cleverly*, an adverb, cannot qualify a noun.
5.	✗	**Any** women were dancing on the floor.
	✓	**Some** women were dancing on the floor.
	C	*Any* usually carries a negative sense. It means *anyone* and cannot go with a plural noun *women*.
6.	✗	He never gave me **some** food.
	✓	He never gave me **any** food.
	C	In a negative sentence we use *any* rather than *some*.
7.	✗	**Few** people can do what they want in life.
	✓	**A few** people can do what they want in life.
	C	*Few* means 'hardly any' whereas '*a few*' means 'some'.
8.	✗	I have to buy **any** articles from the market.

	✓	I have to buy **some** articles from the market.
	C	In positive sense, we use **some** rather than **any**.
9.	✗	I will not eat **something**.
	✓	I will not eat **anything**.
	C	In a negative sentence we use the quantifier **any** rather than **some**.
10.	✗	Have you **some** of the books that we borrowed from the library yesterday?
	✓	Have you **any** of the books that we borrowed from the library yesterday?
	C	In questions **any** is used, as a quantifier, though in some context, **some** is used (e.g Will you have **some** tea?)
11.	✗	**Little** knowledge can be dangerous.
	✓	A little knowledge can be dangerous.
	C	Little means 'hardly any' and *a little* means some amount of.
12.	✗	A **little** persons donated for the needy.
	✓	**A few** persons donated for the needy.
	C	With countable nouns we use *a few* rather than *a little*. Some is used with both mass and countable nouns.
13.	✗	I want **little** milk.

✓ I want **some** milk.

C *Little* is inappropriate because it means 'almost no.'

14. ✗ All the people, who came, were **well**.

✓ All the people, who came, were **good**.

C Where we need a predicative adjective we use *good*; when we need an adverb, we need *well*.

15. ✗ He is very **good**, thank you.

✓ He is very **well**, thank you.

C As in (14).

16. ✗ **Good** begun is half done.

✓ **Well** begun is half done.

C *Well* is the modifier of the verb *begin* here; *Good* cannot be used to modify a verb.

17. ✗ All is **good** that ends **good**.

✓ All is **well** that ends **well**.

C We need the modifier of the verb, i.e. well.

18. ✗ Even without asking, she gave me **many** advice.

✓ Even without asking, she gave me **much** advice.

	C	Advice is a mass noun and needs *much*. *Many* occur with countable nouns.
19.	✗	I reached the ceremony on time **as usually**.
	✓	I reached the ceremony on time as usual.
	C	Usually means 'as usual' and cannot be used with as (i.e., as usual is wrong).
20.	✗	Too much salt in a dish, makes it taste **bitterly**.
	✓	Too much salt in a dish, makes it taste **bitter**.
	C	Bitter refers to *the dish* and not the verb *taste*. Bitterly can refer only to the verb.
21.	✗	He is used to talking **much** nonsense.
	✓	He is used to talking **such** nonsense.
	C	Such means 'of the type previously mentioned' and can be used with *nonsense*. As *nonsense* means 'words which have no sense' it does not make sense to quantify it by much.
22.	✗	Prevention is **good** than cure.
	✓	Prevention is **better** than cure.

	C	As we are comparing **prevention** with **cure**, we have to use the comparative marker than.
23.	✗	The flowers smell more **sweetly** in the morning.
	✓	The flowers smell more **sweet** in the morning.
	C	**Sweet** is the predicative adjective for **flowers**.
24.	✗	You are actually the **tall** man in the family!
	✓	You are actually the **tallest** man in the family!
	C	As we are comparing all members of the family, **tallest** is the appropriate adjective.
25.	✗	This is the **eldest** monument in the world.
	✓	This is the **oldest** monument in world.
	C	**Eldest** is used in the sense of **oldest** only when we compare close relatives.
26.	✗	This plan is **more better**.
	✓	This plan is **better**.
	C	**Better** is the comparative of **good** and does not need another comparative marker.

27.
- ✗ My boss is senior **than** me by five years.
- ✓ My boss is senior **to** me by five years.
- C The comparative forms *senior* and *junior* take *to* rather *than*.

28.
- ✗ Sam is junior **than** me.
- ✓ Sam is junior **to** me.
- C As explained earlier.

29.
- ✗ The quality of this bed is inferior **than** that.
- ✓ The quality of this bed is inferior to that.
- C *Inferior* and superior take to (rather than **than**) as the comparative marker.

30.
- ✗ I prefer bread **than** rice.
- ✓ I prefer bread **to** rice.
- C Prefer is followed by the preposition *to*, and not **than**.

31.
- ✗ Have you met the **eldest** woman of the village?
- ✓ Have you met the **oldest** woman of the village?
- C *Eldest* is used only when we are comparing the members of the same family.

Little Red Book of Common Errors

32. ❌ He is **better** talented than any other man.

✓ He is ***more** talented* than any other man.

C ***Better*** is the comparative of ***good***. The comparative of *talented* will be more talented.

33. ❌ This is the **best** of the two options available.

✓ This is **better** of the two options available.

C As we are comparing only two options, we have to use ***better***.

34. ❌ Rita and Natasha are sisters. The latter is elder **than** Rita.

✓ Rita and Natasha are sisters. The latter is elder **to** Rita.

C ***Elder*** and ***younger*** are followed by ***to***, and not ***than***.

35. ❌ This is the last that I can do for you.

✓ This is the least that I can do for you.

C ***Least*** means 'smallest amount' whereas ***last*** means 'final'. ***Last*** is inappropriate in this context.

36. ❌ **Whole** country was celebrating its independence.

✓ **The whole** country was celebrating its independence.

	C	The expression ***whole country*** has a countable noun as its head. As it is a definite expression, it must have ***the*** preceding it, and not a.
37.	**✗**	We can give you an appointment only for **Sunday next**.
	✓	We can give you an appointment only for **next Sunday**.
	C	The qualifier ***next*** must precede the noun ***Sunday***. In almost all cases, adjectives precede the nouns they qualify.
38.	**✗**	Ruby is **precious** than any other stone.
	✓	Ruby is **more precious** than any other stone.
	C	As there is a comparison between ruby and ***any other stone***, we must have the comparative marker ***than*** between them.
39.	**✗**	**Rich** should not look down upon **poor**.
	✓	**The rich** should not look down upon **the poor**.
	C	When adjectives are used as common (generic) nouns, they are ***preceded by the***.

WHY ADVERBS GO WRONG

1. ✗ Hardly had I left it rained.

   ✓ Hardly had I left **before it** rained.

   C The two clauses *I had left* and *it rained* need to be formally joined (as here by before).

2. ✗ The butter melted quite **fastly** in the sun.

   ✓ The butter melted quite **fast** in the sun.

   C *Fast* can be used as an adverb. There is no adverb form *fastly*.

3. ✗ She sang **lovely**.

   ✓ She sang **a lovely song**.

   C *Lovely* is an adjective and can be used only to qualify a noun (e.g. *song*).

4. ✗ The performance was **mostly over**, when I reached.

   ✓ The performance was **almost over**, when I reached.

   C *Almost* means 'very nearly' whereas *mostly* means 'usually'.

5. ✗ After lunch, we slept **good**.

   ✓ After lunch, we slept **well**.

   C *Well* is used to modify the verb sleep's good, is an adjective.

6.
- ✗ We must never think **bad** of anyone.
- ✓ We must never think **ill** of anyone.
- C As an adverb, *ill* means 'badly' or 'wrongly'. *Bad* cannot be used as an adverb.

7.
- ✗ He fared quite **bad** in the first paper.
- ✓ He fared quite **badly** in the first paper.
- C *Badly* is an adverb which modifies *fared*. The adjective cannot do so.

8.
- ✗ She was looking quite **good** and healthy after the break she took.
- ✓ She was looking quite **well** and healthy after the break she took.
- C One looks *well* but appears to be *good*. Well is an adverb which modifies the verb *look*. *Good* refers to a noun or pronoun.

9.
- ✗ Do you always read so **fastly**?
- ✓ Do you always read so **fast**?
- C *Fast* is an adjective as well as an adverb. As an adverb, it modifies *read*.

10.
- ✗ He plays chess **good**.
- ✓ He plays chess **well**.
- C *Well* modifies the verb *plays*; adjective cannot do so.

Little Red Book of Common Errors 179

11. ✗ I **do not hardly** thought about it.

    ✓ I **hardly** thought about it.

    C *Hardly* means 'scarcely' or come to an insignificant degree'. It carries a negative sense.

12. ✗ I **did not scarcely** hear him.

    ✓ I **did scarcely** hear him.

    C *Scarcely* means *rarely* and carries a negative sense. It is not used in a negative sentence.

13. ✗ He is **most smart** of the two.

    ✓ He is **smarter** of the two.

    C As only two persons are involved, the comparative degree is to be used.

14. ✗ I looked for my books everywhere, but could not find it **nowhere**.

    ✓ I looked for my books everywhere, but could not find **them anywhere**.

    C *Nowhere* means 'not any where'. We can say *I could find it nowhere*.

15. ✗ I went through the books **quick**.

    ✓ I went through the books **quickly**.

    C *Quick* is an adjective whereas *quickly* is an adverb and modifies find.

16. ✗ He went **hurry so that** he could catch her.

	✓	He went **hurriedly** so that he could catch her.
	C	*Hurry* can be used as a verb or a noun. Its adverbial form is *hurriedly*.
17.	✗	I could not **help not** enjoying the play.
	✓	I could not **help** enjoying the play.
	C	We don't use two negatives in a sentence; *could not help* means 'could not stop oneself from'.
18.	✗	Your notes are **equally as good as** mine.
	✓	Your notes are **as good** as mine.
	C	'*As good as*' means '*equally good*' and the use of equally is unnsary.
19.	✗	**Repeat again what** you have said.
	✓	**Repeat what** you have said.
	C	*Repeat* means '*to say again*' and the use of *again* is unnecessary.
20.	✗	They all wished me **good**.
	✓	They all wished me **well**.
	C	The sentence needs an adverb (i.e., *well*) and not an adjective (i.e. good).
21.	✗	The flowers were **beautiful** laid out.
	✓	The flowers were **beautifully** laid out.

	C	*Laid out* is a verbal expression and needs an adverb (i.e. *beautifully*) rather than an adjective.
22.	✗	This dress **is equally** as valuable as that one.
	✓	This dress **is as** valuable as that one.
	C	'*As valuable as*' means *equally valuable* and the use of *equally* is redundant.
23.	✗	The dog is still **live**.
	✓	The dog is still **alive**.
	C	*Alive* means 'having life' and *live* as an adjective means 'not dead, living'. In the predicative use, *alive* is used as a qualifier.
24.	✗	He works **hard** than his brother.
	✓	He works **harder** than his brother.
	C	When two situations are compared, we use the comparative form of the adverb, e.g *harder*.
25.	✗	He has **much** money than all of us.
	✓	He has **more** money than all of us.
	C	The comparative form of *much* is *more*. We need a comparative form here.
26.	✗	I have looked **all places**.
	✓	I have looked **everywhere**.

Little Red Book of Common Errors

	C	*Everywhere* means 'in all places'. The first sentence needs in.
27.	✗	She is angry with him **still**.
	✓	She is **still** angry with him.
	C	*Still* modifies angry and must precede it.
28.	✗	The hospital **yet is not** open.
	✓	The hospital is **not yet** open.
	C	*Yet* (meaning *still*) modifies open and must be adjacent to it.
29.	✗	Never before **I had** seen such a show.
	✓	Never before **had I** seen such a show.
	C	Where a sentence begins with *never* (*before*) the auxiliary verb precedes its subject.

PREPOSITIONS THAT PUZZLE

1.	✗	Do you know the man I spoke **with**?
	✓	Do you know the man I spoke **to**?
	C	*Speak* to is a phrasal verb which means 'to talk in order to give or obtain information'.
2.	✗	This is the house we used to play **on**.
	✓	This is the house we used to play **in**.

| C | One usually plays inside a house, not **on** it. |

3.
✗	Here is the girl you were enquiring **of**.
✓	Here is the girl you were enquiring **about**.
C	*Enquire* takes the preposition *about* when it means 'ask information about someone'.

4.
✗	What was that woman looking **in**?
✓	What was that woman looking **at**?
C	We *look at* something when we gaze in a specified direction. *Look into* means 'investigate'. There is no plural verb *look in*.

5.
✗	It has been raining **from** two days.
✓	It has been raining **for** two days.
C	For a duration of time we use *for*; *from* is used with the starting point of the duration if the end point is also suggested.

6.
✗	I have been living in India **from** 1934.
✓	I have been living at India **since** 1934.
C	As we have a starting point of the duration of time, we use since.

7. ✗ He has been sleeping **since** two hours.

   ✓ He has been sleeping **for** two hours.

   C ***Two hours*** indicates duration and needs ***for***.

8. ✗ They have been drinking **since** an hour.

   ✓ They have been drinking **for** an hour.

   C An hour suggests a duration without a starting point and needs ***for***.

9. ✗ I have been going to class **from** Wednesday.

   ✓ I have been going to class **since** Wednesday.

   C ***Wednesday*** suggests a fixed starting point of time and there is no end point, hence we need ***since***.

10. ✗ I shall be regular **since** March.

    ✓ I shall be regular **from** March.

    C There is a starting point of time and the end point is implied, hence we used ***from***.

11. ✗ The seminar begins **since** 8 December.

    ✓ The seminar begins **from** 8 December.

12.
- ✗ Divide the clothes **between** all these children.
- ✓ Divide the clothes **among** all these children.
- C Between is used when only two parties are involved, ***among*** when three or more parties are involved.

13.
- ✗ They divided the property **between** themselves.
- ✓ They divided the property **among** themselves.
- C If ***themselves*** means more than two ***among*** will be used. See (12).

14.
- ✗ We travelled on a train and he **on** a plane.
- ✓ We travelled by a train and he **by** a plane.
- C Whe we travel by means of a conveyance we use the preposition ***by***.

15.
- ✗ He likes to travel **by** horseback.
- ✓ He likes to travel **on** horseback.
- C As we ride ***on*** a horse, we travel on ***horseback***, not ***by horseback***.

16.
- ✗ They went to school **by** foot.

186 *Little Red Book of Common Errors*

	✓	They went to school **on** foot.
	C	With *foot* we use the preposition 'on'.
17.	✗	Don't you know how to ride **in a** bicycle?
	✓	Don't you know how to ride **a** bicycle?
	C	We ride *on* a bicycle, not inside it.
18.	✗	Travelling **in air** is generally safer.
	✓	Travelling **by air** is generally safer.
	C	*By air* means by an airplane, See earlier.
19.	✗	They suddenly got **of** the bus.
	✓	They suddenly got **off** the bus.
	C	*Off* means 'moving away from' or 'down from' (the bus, etc.).
20.	✗	Early in bed, early to rise.
	✗	Rita went **in** sea alone.
	✓	Early to bed, early **to** rise.
	✓	Rita went to sea alone.
	C	Before we are *in bed*, we *go to bed*.
21.	✗	He was **in** office.
	✓	He was **at** office.
	C	*At office* is a fixed expression where *office* may refer to a noun, a set of

22. ✗ She went **into** their house.

    ✓ She went **to** their house.

    C We go *from* a starting point *to* a destination (e.g., a house).

23. ✗ He struggled **in** the whole month.

    ✓ He struggled **for** the whole month.

    C *The whole month* indicates duration without a starting point and needs *for*.

24. ✗ It gets very hot **in** the summers.

    ✓ It gets very hot **during** the summers.

    C *During* is used for a period of time; it means 'throughout the duration of'. In expresses a point or point of time during which something happens.

25. ✗ We look forward **up** your arrival.

    ✓ We look forward **to** your arrival.

    C *Look forward* is always followed by to, and not by *up*. It is because *forward* suggests further movements.

26. ✗ They set **on** late in the evening.

    ✓ They set **out** late in the evening.

    C *To set out* means 'to begin a journey' or 'intend to do something', whereas set on means 'to attack someone violently. The latter is inappropriate in this context.

27. ✗ I have given **out** looking at birds.

✓ I have given **up** looking at birds.

C To *give up* means to 'cause making an effort' whereas to *give out* means 'to be completely useed up' or 'to speak in anger'. The latter is inappropriate in this context.

28. ✗ A boy jumped **in** the stream.

✓ A boy jumped **into** the stream.

C **In** suggests that something is in the enclosure, *into* means going from outside to inside the enclosure.

29. ✗ They invited all of us **for** dinner.

✓ They invited all of us **to** dinner.

C *To invite* means 'to request some *to* go somewhere or do something'.

30. ✗ He is anxious **about** his daughter's marriage.

✓ He is anxious **for** his daughter's marriage.

C One is always anxious *for* (worried about)

31. ✗ Why are you angry **by** me?

✓ Why are you angry **with** me?

	C	One is angry *with* a person *about* something.
32.	✗	His mother was enraged **with** his stupid question.
	✓	His mother was enraged **at** his stupid question.
	C	One is *enraged* at someone or something.
33.	✗	He gave a talk suitable **to** the occasion.
	✓	He gave a talk suitable **for** the occasion.
	C	*Suitable* is followed by *for*.
34.	✗	I had a long discussion **by** her.
	✓	I had a long discussion **with** her.
	C	One has a discussion *with* someone *on* something.
35.	✗	I am very grateful **for** your family.
	✓	I am very grateful **to** your family.
	C	One is grateful *to* someone *for* something.
36.	✗	He was married **with** Natasha.
	✓	He was married **to** Natasha.

| | C | One *is* or *gets married* to someone. |

37.
	✗	Copy this report word **by** word.
	✓	Copy this report word **for** word.
	C	***Word for word*** means 'in exactly the same way'. ***Word by word*** is not an informative expression.

38.
	✗	Do not compare a rose **to** a lotus.
	✓	Do not compare a rose **with** a lotus.
	C	We always compare someone or something ***with*** someone (or something) else.

39.
	✗	Give me a chair to **sit**.
	✓	Give me a chair to **sit on**.
	C	One sits *on* (or *in*) a chair. By itself, *sit* means 'to cause to be in a sitting position'.

40.
	✗	I have no pencil to **draw**.
	✓	I have no pencil to **draw with**.
	C	Since *pencil* is used an instrument for drawing, it must have a preposition, i.e., *with* to connect it to the verb.

41.
| | ✗ | Don't interfere **with** my mother's affairs. |
| | ✓ | Don't interfere **in** my mother's affairs. |

	C	*Interfere* is always followed by the preposition *in*.
42.	✗	My father deals **with** guns.
	✓	My father deals **in** guns.
	C	*Deals in* refers to *buy* and *sell* whereas *deal with* means 'to discuss'.
43.	✗	Many people died **in** cold.
	✓	Many people died **of** cold.
	C	A person or an animal dies (i.e. stops living) *of* some disease.
44.	✗	I read it **on** a magazine.
	✓	I read it **in** a magazine.
	C	The reference is to some content *inside* a magazine.
45.	✗	What do you know **of** this accident?
	✓	What do you know **about** this accident?
	C	We know *about* some event or have the knowledge *of* that thing.
46.	✗	Harry is confident **on** my success.
	✓	Harry is confident **of** my success.
	C	One can show confidence *in* someone *but* be confident *of* something.
47.	✗	This can happen with anybody.

	✓	This can happen to anybody.
	C	***Happen to*** means 'be experienced by'. Something may happen to someone.
48.	✗	I am not at all familiar by the text.
	✓	I am not at all familiar with the text.
	C	***To be familiar with*** means 'to have a good knowledge of'. It is a fixed expression.
49.	✗	Did you participate with the wrestling competition?
	✓	Did you participate in the wrestling competition?
	C	One always participates (i.e. takes part) in some activity
50.	✗	I prefer fresh lime water than cold drinks.
	✓	I prefer fresh lime water to cold drinks.
	C	Prefer needs to, and no other preposition, so does preference (to).
51.	✗	I should receive what is due on me.
	✓	I should receive what is due to me.
	C	With due (in the sence of something that is moral or legal obligation) *to* is used.
52.	✗	They fought on the injustice.

| ✓ | They fought against the injustice. |
| C | If one fights to achieve something, we use *for*, if we strive to oppose or stop something, we use *against*. |

53.
✗	You cannot prevent him of getting the job.
✓	You cannot prevent him from getting the job.
C	Prevent means 'to stop something from happening', and is followed by from.

54.
✗	I thank all of you by behalf of my family and me.
✓	I thank all of you on behalf of my family and me.
C	The phrase is **on behalf of**. It is an invariable expression.

55.
✗	Soon they got on their difficulties.
✓	Soon they got over their difficulties.
C	***Got over*** means 'overcome' or 'recover from'; ***got on*** means 'continue doing something'. The latter is inappropriate in this context.

56.
| ✗ | One must try to live in his or her modest means. |
| ✓ | One must try to live **within** his or her modest means. |

	C	***Within*** means inside the range of an area or boundary whereas ***in*** suggests the situation of something inside something else. In this context, ***within*** is more appropriate.
57.	✗	Is this water fit **to** drinking?
	✓	Is this water fit **for** drinking?
	C	***Fit*** means 'suitable' and is followed by ***for***.
58.	✗	He ran **over** the street in a hurry.
	✓	He ran **across** the street in a hurry.
	C	***Run across*** means 'pass quickly from one side to the other' whereas ***run over*** (in this context of driving) means 'to knock a person and pass over his body'.
59.	✗	When I saw him, he was shivering by cold.
	✓	When I saw him, he was shivering with cold.
	C	***To shiver*** means 'to shake uncontrollably as a result of being cold (frightened or excited). If is followed by ***with***.
60.	✗	You must pay the fine by a week.
	✓	You must pay the fine within a week.
	C	***Within*** a week draws the boundary of

time. Which by a week does not; **by** indicates the dead line of a particular time period.

61. ✗ The candle will not be able to last **by** the night.

    ✓ The candle will not be able to last **through** the night.

    C *By* indicates a period within which something happens, *through* suggests continuing in time towards completion of a process.

62. ✗ He is suffering **with** cough.

    ✓ He is suffering **from** cough.

    C ***To suffer from*** means to be afflicted by a disease. It is a phrasal expression.

63. ✗ I purchased this furniture **in** an auction.

    ✓ I purchased this furniture **at** an auction.

    C *At* indicates 'a point of location' *in* an area. The latter is not intended here.

64. ✗ There was no cash **by** him.

    ✓ There was no cash **on** him.

    C ***To have cash on*** someone is an idiomatic expression it is fixed.

65. ✗ It is **among** you and me.

- ✓ It is **between** you and me.
- C When something involves two parties we use *between*. *Among* is used for three or more.

66.
- ✗ What is the time in your watch?
- ✓ What is the time by your watch?
- C By *one's watch* is an invariable idiomatic expression.

67.
- ✗ The pillow is **upon** the bed.
- ✓ The pillow is **on** the bed.
- C Both *on* and *upon* suggest the same position but *upon* is used in only formal contexts.

CONTRADICTION OF CONJUNCTIONS

1.
- ✗ Look carefully, else you will **not miss** the plane.
- ✓ Look carefully, else you will **miss** the plane.
- C (*Or*) *else* is used as a conjunction to signal that the second clause is contrary to the first.

2.
- ✗ Neither a borrower **or** a lender can ever live in peace.
- ✓ Neither a borrower **nor** a lender can ever live in peace.

	C	***Neither*** is paired by ***nor*** (and not ***or***). Together they negative both the clauses.
3.	✗	You must jump now **either** you will miss the opportunity.
	✓	You must jump now **or** you will miss the opportunity.
	C	***Either*** is used before the first of the two alternatives, or before the second in the positive sentences.
4.	✗	They were wounded **but** they carried on.
	✓	They were wounded **still** they carried on.
	C	***But*** indicates that the second clause is contrary to expectation of ***still***, means 'even then'.
5.	✗	Although it is not raining, **but** I shall take my umbrella.
	✓	Although it is not raining, **yet** I shall take my umbrella.
	C	***Yet*** as a conjunction means 'nevertheless'.
6.	✗	He will not come unless **you don't** call him.
	✓	He will not come unless **you** call him.
	C	Unless (except if) is used to introduce a clause which is not true or valid.

7. ✗ You will fail unless **you don't** take his notes.

   ✓ You will fail unless **you** take his notes.

   C See earlier.

8. ✗ Scarcely had I finished my food **than** she called me.

   ✓ Scarcely had I finished my food **when** she called me.

   C The first clause mentions a point of time which is represented by *when* in the second. There is no comparison involved. *Scarcely* means 'only just', and *when* means 'at that time'.

9. ✗ Anybody would scarcely believe me, **if** I say I attended the party thrown by him.

   ✓ Anybody would scarcely believe me, **when** I say I attended the party thrown by him.

   C As an adverb *scarcely* means 'hardly'. *When* means at that time. It makes the statement conditional and should not be used if that is not intended.

10. ✗ Unless **you don't** show me the results, I shall not rely on you.

    ✓ Unless **you** show me results, I shall not rely on you.

	C	The second clause makes sense only when the first is positive.
11.	✗	Be careful lest you **do not** fall in the gutter.
	✓	Be careful lest you **should** fall in the gutter.
	C	When *lest* is used after a clause it suggests fear. It is used with the intrusion of preventing something undesirable.
12.	✗	Run fast lest you **do not miss** her.
	✓	Run fast lest you **miss** her.
	C	See earlier.
13.	✗	Supposing **if it** rains, would you go out?
	✓	Supposing **it** rains, would you go out?
	C	As both *supposing* and *if* indicate a condition, only one of them should be used.
14.	✗	Until you **do not come**, I shall wait for you here on this doorstep.
	✓	Until you **come**, I shall wait for you here on this doorstep.
	C	As a conjunction, *until* refers to the point of time, mentioned in the clause.
15.	✗	I like neither him **or** her.

✓ I like neither him **nor** her.

> C In negative sentences as we use *neither*... nor, in positive sentences, *either* - or.

16. ✗ I don't know whether he **likes** this.

✓ I don't know whether he **will like** this or not.

> C Since the embedded clause is a prediction, the future is used appropriately.

17. ✗ I was **too** glad when I saw him yesterday.

✓ I was **very** glad when I saw him yesterday.

> C As an intensifier, *too* suggests that the adjective used is excessive which is not appropriate here.

18. ✗ She is intelligent and beautiful **to**.

✓ She is intelligent and beautiful **too**.

> C *To* is a preposition whereas too here means 'in addition'.

19. ✗ He ran very fast and **he** won the race.

✓ He ran very fast and (**therefore**) won the race.

> C Since *he* is the subject in both the

clauses, its repetition is unnecessary

20. ✗ He ate for he wanted to eat, **but** for he liked eating.

✓ He ate **not because** he wanted to eat, **but because** he liked eating.

C When used as a conjunction, *for* means 'because' but here we need *not* (only) because and *but* (also) *because* to include and emphasize both the reasons.

21. ✗ I did not get married and she did not get married.

✓ I did not get married and she did not either.

C *Either* is used alone in a negative sentence to suggest similarity with the first clause.

22. ✗ I went and she went.

✓ I went and she went too.

C *Too*, (as an adverb) means *also* and is emphatic.

23. ✗ He is too weak in talking.

✓ He is too weak to talk.

C *Too*, as the modifier of an adjective, means 'to a higher degree than is desirable'.

24. ✗ They as well as he is to blame.

They as well as he are to blame.

As well means 'in addition to'. **As well as** is used like **and**. Since the sentence has two subjects, the verb must be plural.